to Sy
Dr. Norm
(Uncle Norm)

What Has Happened To
My Church?

A Challenge To The 21st Century Churches

Written and Published by

Dr. Norman P. Anderson

First Published in November, 2015

1

Table of Contents

Scripture quotations are from
the New King James Version

Prologue: Why This Book?

I n my observation of evangelical churches, the biblical health of the Western-world church is declining. The growing number of mega-churches gives the impression that they are doing something right. When mega-churches can draw thousands of people on a Sunday morning, does this not indicate good spiritual health and solid biblical foundations? Would God's blessing be upon them if they were not worthy of His blessing?

This conclusion assumes that numbers is the criteria of God's favor and approval. This premise is completely untrue. Size has no bearing upon the integrity of God's church and the favor of the Lord toward a congregation of believers. Largeness or smallness is not proof that a local church is biblical or that it is fulfilling its mission given by the Lord Jesus who is the builder of His church.

George Barna, in his research, wrote the following:

> Our research discovered that when Protestant churches attempt to evaluate their success, one of the primary elements they gauge is attendance. Rather than evaluate spiritual growth, most churches settle for measuring numerical growth, even though a variety of studies have shown there is little correlation between those two metrics.[1]

---

[1] George Barna, Futurecast (Carol Stream, Illinois: Barna Books,, 2011), page 183

The culture of the Western world has undergone the most rapid period of change in the last twenty years that has ever occurred in the history of the world. Technology has advanced so rapidly that it is almost impossible to keep up with the pace of the change. Pastors and other leaders of the churches have sought to adapt to the changing culture in order to more effectively reach the people of this generation.

The church growth movement of the last forty five years has brought some good things to the attention of church leaders. However, it has also done a disservice to the church as well. I have my Doctor of Ministry degree in church growth and therefore I have sufficient knowledge of this movement to make an evaluation of its strengths and weaknesses.

Here are some of the strengths of this movement.

The leaders of this movement served to shake some evangelical churches out of their complacency regarding evangelism and outreach. Studies showed that additions to the local church were predominantly the result of transfer from other churches rather than new believers in Christ.

The church growth movement also developed an awareness of methods that would make the church more appealing to the non-churched in our communities. Developing awareness of our buildings and their attractiveness, having friendly greeters and parking lot attendants, and educating church members to being sensitive to new visitors were all positive helps to a church's impact in a community. Involvement in community life by serving the community in practical ways increased the authenticity of a local church's 'salt and light' impact.

The church growth movement has led churches to reconsider their purpose and mission. In some churches it has produced intentionality when it comes to the task of evangelism and the outreach of God's redeemed people. It has led to an arousal from slumber when it comes to our efforts to be the Lord's light in our darkened world.

Here are some of the weaknesses that have led to the decline of the evangelical churches biblically.

Church growth leaders say: "Methods must change but the message remains the same." This is not always true of the evangelical churches. The message has often been compromised or weakened by the desire not to offend the people who come to participate in our services.

The church's desire to be acceptable to the unsaved has often led to the silence of the church about the culture in which we find ourselves. The declining moral culture in our western world and the pressure to conform and to be politically correct, has often produced a weakened church. It has often led to compromise of God's revealed truth.

The emphasis upon numbers has led to much change in the format and the worship of many churches. Too often the desire to attract 'non-church Charlie' has led to compromise of the message and to a false sense of security in the lives of many non-repentant "believers." The philosophy of worship and the teaching of the biblical definition of 'church' requires much rethinking and reform.

Many of God's people are troubled over the condition of evangelical churches today.

Do you hear the bleating of the sheep? I have sought to summarize some of the 'bleatings' that I found on one Internet blog site.

Sandra, a very mobile person, after visiting a lot of churches says, "I'm seeing the worldliness of the churches . . . but I also see the politically correct pastors who aren't willing to step up and tell it like it is."

Political correctness is ruining our society. Pastors must not succumb to political correctness when it comes to the proclamation of God's word.

Gene comments about three pastors, who followed a very good pastor, "each of whom split the church apart. The third of these pastors dressed sloppily, brought many changes to the format of worship, including coffee-house style, and told the older believers if they didn't like it, they should leave."

Wisdom is needed in bringing necessary change. Change must be gradual and wisely implemented. Is it necessary and wise to go from suits and ties to sloppy cargo pants and a t-shirt? Pastors ought to consider the feelings of their people and love them. When people feel they are loved and cared for, they are more likely to accept some changes, especially when they understand the reasons for the changes.

Greg asks, "Where are the churches that sing hymns? When did we stop singing hymns? Not only do we not have the opportunity to sing traditional songs, we aren't supposed to ask questions about why not."

Eunice says, "When they started letting this so called 'Christian rock' into the services, it went from bad to worse and eventually they stopped singing hymns. Now I don't even know the songs they put out there. I love the Bill Gaither music type of songs, something that touches the heart."

Wanda shares her heart, "In the still of the night when I lay down to sleep and find sleep not immediate, it is the words of the songs that I learned as a little girl that usher me into the rest the dark offers."

Music is a big contentious issue. Many of the older generation and also a few of the younger generation love the traditional hymns of the church. Some churches offer a "traditional" service; however it is usually early on Sunday morning rather than the traditional time. Older people with all the maladies of aging find it very challenging to get up and get moving for an 8 A.M. service.

Wanda comments further,

> I'm seventy two, working on seventy three, and have COPD from many issues lived through over those years. I don't attend the church as often as I once did. My tithes are paid forward regularly though in support of God's work. I am on the mailing list where I get their flyers, so I know they receive my check each month. I get an accounting of the amount at the end of the year. My husband died 11 years ago and that is the last time any of those members have been in my home. . . I wonder why . . . I have three different ministers I watch from the televised sermons each Sunday and I truly appreciate them and

often think maybe I should be sending them my tithes instead of where my membership lies. I read my Bible, I have friends I stay encouraged by and offer them my compassion but I don't know what happened to my church . . . It grew bigger and relocated to accommodate that growth . . . guess I stood still behind a wall too long, or maybe I grew too old and slow to keep up.

Do you hear the bleating of a neglected sheep? In the light of James' words that pure and undefiled religion is about visiting widows and orphans, isn't it sad that this lady has not had a visit in eleven years?[2]

Catherine offers, "I just left a huge growing church with a pastor who is a great speaker but not a great preacher. If I wanted motivational speaking and feel good stuff, I'd spend the money and do a weekend seminar. We need more scripture based teaching."

Justin notes: "The problem with all the churches around me are they are too worldly. The messages are not teaching, the pastors are too worried about trying to be funny or like Joel Osteen. They are tuned into the club atmosphere, and the message of the Bible gets lost. Another problem I see is that churches today are not teaching morals or values. The anything-goes, casual worship does not build disciples of Christ; it takes away from the message and the seriousness of sin."

Lila shares, "Because of health reasons I don't go to church services as often as I did before, but also I find that the meaning of "church" has changed considerably from the past. In my opinion there is not as much caring and concern for the sick,

---

[2] James 1:23

widowed, disabled and poor members as there was before . . . Music has become repetitious and boring and the feeling of awe and holiness has left for entertainment instead. There is too much catering to the unchurched which has caused, in my opinion, compromising with the world regarding the music, activities and teaching. The strong teaching of the Word is seldom taught for fear of offending, so the gospel has been watered down and has become ineffective."

While some of these comments might be considered a bit extreme, it is time for pastors and other church leaders to listen carefully. Do not write these people off as being old-fashioned or simply opposed to change. They represent many thousands, perhaps even hundreds of thousands of Christians who are crying out for biblically based churches. Can you hear their hearts crying out for some love and compassion? Do you hear hungry sheep bleating to be fed the word of the Lord?

In our evangelical churches, a great number of our pastors are suffering because they sense that they are failing to live up to the expectations placed upon them. John S. Dickerson comments:

> Leaders are crumbling, often silently and internally, under the pressures of late-20th-century ministry. Each year pastors suffer heart attacks, strokes, emotional breakdowns, divorces, and bankruptcies from the strain of this religious system. Many more manage to keep the pressures unknown and internalized.[3]

Dickerson also comments on the declining numbers of evangelicals and the marginalization of evangelical churches in America.

---

[3] John S. Dickerson, The Great Evangelical Recession, (Baker Books, Grand Rapids, Michigan, 2013), page 185

He defines an "evangelical" as a person who believes the Bible is totally trustworthy and that Jesus is the only way to the Father and heaven. He cites studies indicating that our numbers in America today total only seven to nine percent of the population, less than one in ten. If current trends continue, within thirty years we will be one in twenty five.

Dickerson also finds in his studies that two-thirds of church-going young adults are leaving the church by the age of thirty; and two-thirds of them will never come back. Among Millennials (ages eighteen to twenty nine), there are four to six times as many atheists, agnostics, and non-religious people as there are evangelicals. Clearly, our faith has become marginal to our society.

These young people are hungry for something that satisfies the emptiness of their hearts and souls. Some churches, in their well-intentioned desire to reach them, have so failed in preaching the meat of God's Word that these young folks go away still hungry and hurting.

So we must take a long look and consider the direction the evangelical churches are moving. We must allow pastors to be biblically-based pastors, following the directions of their Master.

In 2 Thessalonians 2, the apostle Paul speaks of the coming of the Antichrist in the last days. In verse three, he speaks of 'the falling away' that must come before the disclosure of the Antichrist. It is possible that we are in that period of time when the decline of the Church of Jesus Christ is preparing the world for the acceptance of the rule of this evil dictator called the Antichrist.

Even if this is so, the followers of Jesus Christ must not simply rollover and accept the decline of the church as inevitable. We must not merely reflect our decaying culture.

It is still incumbent that we seek the Lord with all our heart, mind and strength. The churches must remain true to the word of God and stand true to our Lord and Master, no matter what the cost may be.

My desire and my prayer is that the Lord will be gracious and send revival to the church of Jesus Christ. If there is ever a time for Christian leaders and all Christians to stand up and be counted in a world that is declining into the darkness, it is now. If our churches and our pastors fail us in this challenge, the Lord's judgment will be upon us.

"If the foundations are destroyed, what can the righteous do?" Psalm 11:3.

Chapter 1

A Diagnostic Exam of the 21st Century Church

The church in North America is in trouble! The evangelical church in the Western World is in free fall! I fear that the Lord may be writing Ichabod[4] over many of our congregations.

I visit many congregations and leave without sensing that I have met with God. Why does the Spirit of the Lord seem absent?

Does God find our offerings that we call worship acceptable? Is this too harsh a judgment, perhaps the ranting of an aged pastor, out of touch and unable to adjust to change? May the Lord forgive me if that be true!

A much younger man than I commented about a church experience he had just endured: "I feel like I have been to a pizza party instead of a church service!" Another said "If I wanted a rock concert, I wouldn't go to church to find it!"

David Platt in his book "Radical", tells of the time when he became the pastor of the church at Brook Hills in Birmingham, Alabama. Some would refer

---

[4] "Ichabod is the name of the baby born to the widow of Phineas, one of the sons of Eli. 1 Samuel 4 tells of the capture of the Ark of the Covenant, and the disaster of the defeat of Israel by the Philistines. It led to the death of Eli's sons, Hophni and Phineas, and also the death of Eli, the priest. "Ichabod" means, "the glory has departed from Israel."

to him as "the youngest mega-church pastor in history." Pastor Platt writes as follows:

> Authors I respect greatly, would make statements such as, 'Decide how big you want your church to be, and go for it, whether that's five, ten, or twenty thousand members.' Soon my name was near the top of the list of pastors of the fastest growing U.S. churches. There I was . . . living out the American church dream.

> But I found myself becoming uneasy. For one thing, my model in ministry. He is a guy who spent the majority of his ministry time with twelve men. A guy who, when he left this earth, had only about 120 people who were actually sticking around and doing what he told them to do. More like a mini-church, really. Jesus Christ - the youngest mini-church pastor in history.

As Pastor Platt wrestled with the pathway that he was following, he writes,

> Soon I realized I was on a collision course with an American church culture where success is defined by bigger crowds, bigger budgets, and bigger buildings. I was now confronted with a startling reality: Jesus actually spurned the things that my church culture said were most important.[5]

Like David Platt, it is time for us as pastors and church leaders to seriously and prayerfully question what we are doing in the name of our Lord Jesus

---

[5] Radical, David Platt, (Multnomah Press, Colorado Springs, CO 80921, Copyright 2010) pages 1-2.

Christ and in the name of the church which belongs to Him.

Are we trivializing Almighty God by our offerings which we label worship? Are we really being faithful preachers of the word of God? Are we following the biblical guidelines for the church that are laid out in the New Testament writings? Are we as pastors and church leaders caving into the pressures of modern culture, rather than being faithful to our Master, Jesus Christ? These are tough questions that deserve honest answers!

The prophet, Malachi, begins with the words "The burden of the word of the LORD to Israel by Malachi." My heart is burdened for the church of Jesus Christ. No, I am not claiming that the Lord is inspiring me as He inspired Malachi to write "the word of the LORD." I am not deluded into thinking that I am some special person who has the last word from God about the church. I am simply one of many voices crying in the wilderness for revival from the Lord to come to His church. Many are crying out concerning the lack of power in reaching our current generation.[6]

---

[6] Quote from Dr. Henry M. Morris, (Institute for Creation Research letter, Fall, *2014)* *"During our extensive travels all over North America, ICR has noticed a very real disconnect with Millennials. This generation of young people, commonly identified as those between 18 and 35 years old, are largely absent from many churches we minister to. Those who have not abandoned church altogether have largely deserted "traditional" churches in favor of ultra-contemporary assemblies, many of which have replaced solid expositional teaching with shallow "biblical discussions." Most Christian colleges are in similar straits, and we find the majority of students are sadly ignorant of basic creation doctrine and scientific evidence that confirms the Genesis account. We know that without the conviction that the Bible's very*

The prophet Malachi stung the nation of Israel with his indictment of their worship as he accused them of wearying God and bringing defiled sacrifices. They were deluded into thinking that they were honoring God by their actions.

In Malachi 1:6-14, we read,

A son honors his father, and a servant his master. If then I am the Father, where is My honor? And if I am a Master, where is My reverence?" says the Lord of hosts to you priests who despise My name. Yet you say, 'In what way have we despised Your name?'

You offer defiled food on My altar, but say, 'In what way have we defiled You?' By saying, 'The table of the Lord is contemptible.'

And when you offer the blind as a sacrifice, Is it not evil? And when you offer the lame and sick, is it not evil? Offer it then to your governor! Would he be pleased with you? Would he accept you favorably? says the Lord of hosts.

But now entreat God's favor, that He may be gracious to us. While this is being done by your hands, will He accept you favorably?" says the Lord of hosts.

Who is there even among you who would shut the doors, so that you would not kindle fire on My altar in vain? I have no pleasure in

---

foundation is accurate, many young lives may stumble and choke in their walk and witness for Christ (Matthew 13:2-22)".

you, says the Lord of hosts, Nor will I accept an offering from your hands.

For from the rising of the sun, even to its going down, My name shall be great among the Gentiles; In every place incense shall be offered to My name, And a pure offering; For My name shall be great among the nations, says the Lord of hosts.

But you profane it, in that you say, 'The table of the Lord is defiled; and its fruit, its food, is contemptible.'

You also say, 'Oh, what a weariness!' And you sneer at it, says the Lord of hosts. And you bring the stolen, the lame, and the sick; thus you bring an offering! Should I accept this from your hand?" says the Lord.

But cursed be the deceiver who has in his flock a male, and takes a vow, but sacrifices to the Lord what is blemished - for I am a great King, says the Lord of hosts, and my name is to be feared among the nations.

The Fear of the Lord

The fear of the Lord has disappeared from our churches. Have we so emphasized God's grace, and so misinterpreted the meaning of grace, that we fail to revere His holiness? We come casually into the Presence of the Almighty God without respect and honor. Where can we go to find His awesome Presence? When we gather with God's redeemed people to worship in our modern day evangelical churches, do we sense God's glory, His transcendence? Do we ever ask the question, "Has

God's glory departed from us? Has God written 'Ichabod' over the doors of our churches?"

Proverbs 1:7 says, "The fear of the Lord is the beginning of knowledge, but fools despise wisdom and instruction."

In the Scriptures we read of many who were overwhelmed in the presence of the Lord. They were fearful, trembling in the presence of the Holy God. They feared that the holiness of God would consume them.

Moses is confronted by the very Presence of God in a bush that burned in the desert, yet curiously was not consumed by the flames. Moses drew near to see this unusual site and was startled by the voice of Jehovah speaking to him from the flaming bush. Exodus 3:4-6 reveals the experience of Moses in the very presence of God.

> So when the Lord saw that he turned aside to look, God called to him from the midst of the bush and said, "Moses, Moses!" And he said, "Here I am."

> Then He said, "Do not draw near this place. Take your sandals off your feet, for the place where you stand is holy ground."

> Moreover He said, "I am the God of your father—the God of Abraham, the God of Isaac, and the God of Jacob." And Moses hid his face, for he was afraid to look upon God.

Moses was humbled in the presence of Jehovah, being aware of his unworthiness to be in God's presence. In verse eleven, we read, "But Moses said to God, "Who am I that I should go to Pharaoh, and that I should bring the children of Israel out of Egypt?" Moses sensed his smallness, his insignificance and his inability to serve the Lord."

We also must humble ourselves before our great God and recognize our unworthiness of His grace and mercy. We are so unworthy to be His servants. Then and then only will we truly hear the Lord's response as Moses heard God's voice to him: "I will certainly be with you!"

When Moses received the Ten Commandments from God on Mount Sinai, the people of Israel showed their fear of God as they heard the rumblings from the mountain. The fear of Jehovah was to prevent Israel from sinning against God. The fear of the Lord motivates us to live holy and godly lives. Exodus 20:18-21 tells us about their fear and reverence of God.

> And all the people saw the thunderings, and the lightnings, and the noise of the trumpet, and the mountain smoking: and when the people saw it, they removed, and stood afar off. And they said unto Moses, Speak thou with us, and we will hear: but let not God speak with us, lest we die. And Moses said unto the people, "Fear not: for God is come to prove you, and that His fear may be before your faces that ye sin not. And the people stood afar off, and Moses drew near unto the thick darkness where God was.

The high priest entered before Jehovah in the Holy of holies, behind a veil that separated the people from God's Holy Presence. Once a year on the Day of Atonement, the high priest was commanded to represent the people before the Holy, Almighty God. In Leviticus 16, we find instructions for the

18

high priest to prepare himself by offering a bull in sacrifice for himself and his household. He was to prepare himself by following specific instructions, dressing himself in proper attire, and performing the sacrifice, applying the blood of the substitute sacrifice to the altar. Only then was he prepared to pass behind the veil into the very Presence of Jehovah. He was to take a censer with burning coals from the altar and burn incense as he entered the Holy of holies. The high priest then would apply the blood of the sacrifice, sprinkling it on the Mercy Seat, thus making atonement for himself and the people.

None of this was casual business! It was a very serious and dangerous matter to come into God's holy presence without proper preparation. Such presumption would result in physical death. The high priest and the people of Israel were fearfully aware of the holiness of Jehovah and their utter unworthiness to be in His Presence. Leviticus 16:1-2 says:

> Now the Lord spoke to Moses after the death of the two sons of Aaron, when they offered profane fire before the Lord, and died; and the Lord said to Moses: "Tell Aaron your brother not to come at just any time into the Holy Place inside the veil, before the mercy seat which is on the ark, lest he die; for I will appear in the cloud above the mercy seat.

This ceremonial preparation is not necessary for us who live on this side of the cross of Calvary. Nevertheless we, as believers, must enter the worship of our Lord with the same kind of fear and reverence of His person and His holiness. We are often far too casual and shallow in our worship of our great God, especially in our evangelical churches.

Jesus Christ has borne all of our sin in His own body as He died in our place, taking upon Himself every bit of our guilt. His blood was shed for us to purchase our forgiveness and cleansing. The separating veil in the temple was torn from the top to the bottom when Jesus died. The way to the Holy God was opened once and for all for all sinners who will repent and believe. The writer of Hebrews tells us that we now are to come boldly to the throne of grace.[7]

When we consider this great cost paid by our Savior to rescue us from our sin, we must not come casually, flippantly or irreverently. Every time we gather together in the assembly of believers, we should come with reverence and with fearful awareness of our unworthiness. We must come with grateful worship of our great Savior and Lord. He is the risen Savior, alive forever more. He is the King of kings and the Lord of lords.

The prophet Isaiah went to the temple in a time of desperation and despair. The long reigning King Uzziah had died and Israel was at a crossroad, wondering which way to turn. In his time of grief and uncertainty, Isaiah sought guidance in the temple of the Lord. God revealed Himself in a powerful way to Isaiah and his life was once again renewed by the awesome Presence of the Lord.

Isaiah writes of his experience in Isaiah 6:1-8:

---

[77] Hebrews 4:14-16

In the year that King Uzziah died, I saw the Lord sitting on a throne, high and lifted up, and the train of His robe filled the temple.

Above it stood seraphim; each one had six wings: with two he covered his face, with two he covered his feet, and with two he flew.

And one cried to another and said: "Holy, holy, holy is the Lord of hosts; the whole earth is full of His glory!"

And the posts of the door were shaken by the voice of him who cried out, and the house was filled with smoke.

I said: "Woe is me, for I am undone! Because I am a man of unclean lips, and I dwell in the midst of a people of unclean lips; for my eyes have seen the King, the Lord of hosts."

Then one of the seraphim flew to me, having in his hand a live coal which he had taken with the tongs from the altar. And he touched my mouth with it, and said: "Behold, this has touched your lips; your iniquity is taken away, and your sin purged."

Also I heard the voice of the Lord, saying: "Whom shall I send, and who will go for us?" Then I said, "Here am I! Send me."

Peter, James and John experienced the awesomeness of the Lord Jesus as Jesus led them up onto a high mountain. In Matthew 17, we read that Jesus Christ was transfigured in the awesome Presence of God the Father. We read, "His face shone like the sun, and His clothes became white as the light." Moses and Elijah appeared to them, talking with Jesus.

Peter impulsively responds to the situation with his brilliant idea, or so he thinks. In verse four, "Then Peter answered and said to Jesus, "Lord, it is good for us to be here; if you wish, let us make here three tabernacles: one for You, one for Moses, and one for Elijah." Was Peter simply regarding Jesus on the same plane as Moses and Elijah?

God the Father immediately intervenes. Suddenly the Father speaks in an audible voice out of the cloud, saying "This is my beloved Son, in whom I am well pleased. Hear Him!" Peter's perspective is changed and the three disciples fall on their faces, greatly afraid.[8]

Pentecost was a special time in the life of the fledgling church. In Acts 2, the Holy Spirit comes upon the church and a new day was ushered in with many signs and wonders. The place where they were meeting was filled with a mighty rushing wind that filled the whole house. The result of Pentecost was effective Spirit-filled preaching that led to the repentant faith of about three thousand who believed in Jesus Christ and were baptized that day. Verse forty two tells us that "fear ('phobos' in the Greek text) came upon every soul, and many wonders and signs were done through the apostles."

God's intention in every gathering of believers is that we experience Christ's presence through the Holy Spirit's working in our midst? Do we invoke His special Presence? Do we expect the awesome Presence of God when we gather? While Jesus is always present with us, He has promised a special

---

[8] Matthew 17:6

22

sense of His presence wherever two or three gather together in His name.[9]

Isaiah asks a question that is appropriate for us to consider when we lapse into our casual view of our great God! In Isaiah 40:18: "To whom then will you liken God? Or what likeness will you compare to Him?"

As we gather in His Presence with God's people, Isaiah 40:25-31 leads us to understand the greatness of our God. This great and awesome God acts in behalf of those who wait upon Him.

> "To whom then will you liken Me, or to whom shall I be equal?" says the Holy One.
>
> Lift up your eyes on high, and see who has created these things, Who brings out their host by number; He calls them all by name, by the greatness of His might and the strength of His power; not one is missing.
>
> Why do you say, O Jacob, and speak, O Israel: "My way is hidden from the Lord, and my just claim is passed over by my God"?
>
> Have you not known? Have you not heard? The everlasting God, the Lord, the Creator of the ends of the earth, neither faints nor is weary. His understanding is unsearchable.
> He gives power to the weak, and to those who have no might He increases strength.
>
> Even the youths shall faint and be weary, and the young men shall utterly fall,

---

[9] Matthew 18:20

But those who wait on the Lord shall renew their strength; they shall mount up with wings like eagles, they shall run and not be weary, they shall walk and not faint.

We are always in His Presence and can never escape from His Presence. However, we experience a special sense of the presence of our Lord when we assemble together with other believers that we cannot experience in isolation.

Building Properly on the Foundation

The 'success seminar' has become a crutch for pastors who are seeking to emulate the successful programs of others. Many pastors and church lay leaders are attracted to the seminar put on by the pastor and the church that has been able to be "successful". Pastors traipse off to the seminar hopeful that they will learn the secret that will launch their ministry in a similar way. They return home seeking to implement the new program, only to be disappointed. The numbers do not flock into their church building. Instead they often drive away many people from their congregations, leaving them in despair. There seems to be no other way out of the failure but to resign.

A few succeed in drawing people and they build their bigger church! Those who succeed evaluate their success by the full worship center and believe that it is all because of the Lord's blessing. In some cases, it may be the Lord's blessing upon a biblically sound ministry that is faithful in the gospel and faithful in the preaching of God's word.

However, numbers are not always the sign of God's blessing and God's approval. It is possible to build a "successful" organization through marketing principles and the charisma of an enthusiastic, positive thinking salesman. Are you building wisely on the foundation of the church, Jesus Christ?

As he addresses the carnal, fleshly state of the Corinthian church, the apostle Paul cautions them to be careful how they are building on the foundation. We usually interpret this passage to mean that each of us must build upon Christ, the foundation of our individual lives. However the temple Paul is speaking about in this passage is the church, the corporate body of believers. Give heed to Paul's words in 1 Corinthians 3:1-15.

> And I, brethren, could not speak to you as to spiritual people but as to carnal, as to babes in Christ. I fed you with milk and not with solid food; for until now you were not able to receive it, and even now you are still not able; for you are still carnal. For where there are envy, strife, and divisions among you, are you not carnal and behaving like mere men? For when one says, "I am of Paul," and another, "I am of Apollos," are you not carnal?

> Who then is Paul, and who is Apollos, but ministers through whom you believed, as the Lord gave to each one? I planted, Apollos watered, but God gave the increase. So then neither he who plants is anything, nor he who waters, but God who gives the increase. Now he who plants and he who waters are one, and each one will receive his own reward according to his own labor. For we are God's fellow workers; you are God's field, you are God's building.

> According to the grace of God which was given to me, as a wise master builder I have

laid the foundation, and another builds on it. But let each one take heed how he builds on it. For no other foundation can anyone lay than that which is laid, which is Jesus Christ. Now if anyone builds on this foundation with gold, silver, precious stones, wood, hay, straw, each one's work will become clear; for the Day will declare it, because it will be revealed by fire; and the fire will test each one's work, of what sort it is.

If anyone's work which he has built on it endures, he will receive a reward. If anyone's work is burned, he will suffer loss; but he himself will be saved, yet so as through fire.
Do you not know that you are the temple of God and that the Spirit of God dwells in you? If anyone defiles the temple of God, God will destroy him. For the temple of God is holy, which temple you are.

Every local church is different. Every local setting is different. It is not some program that is the solution. Upon our knees we will find Him Who is the answer. It is incumbent upon every pastor and every church leader to seek diligently for God's Presence and for His wise direction for the local church he has been called to serve. Pastors are called to preach the word of God in the power of the Holy Spirit. They are called to be shepherds of their flocks.

Have we fallen into the trap of Satan? We have brought the world into the church. Many treat the church as simply another business to be run by our own wisdom, our craftiness and our talents. Our approach to ministry is guided by the world's view of success.

Do you long for God to manifest His glory in the assemblies of God's people? Do you long for the experience of standing on holy ground? Do you long for a word from the Lord, spoken from the heart of a pastor who is passionate about what the Lord has given him for his sheep today? Do we stand in the need of revival?

The Purpose of the Gathered Church

As pastors and church leaders we need to reexamine the biblical purpose of the gathered church. Over the last thirty years, we have heard much about the 'seeker sensitive" church. The seeker sensitive church is the church that has sought to make 'unchurched Charlie" feel comfortable when he shows up at church. So pastors are exhorted to go easy on sin and judgment! Don't offend unchurched Charlie with such talk! Don't use theological terms, not even words like 'saved', because he will not understand that term. Keep the sermon short and sweet, so he will be motivated to return to church!

What is the purpose of gathering together as believers? The writer of Hebrews makes it abundantly clear that all believers must faithfully meet together.[10]

> Let us hold fast the confession of our hope without wavering, for He who promised is faithful. And let us consider one another in order to stir up love and good works, not forsaking the assembling of ourselves together, as is the manner of some, but exhorting one another, and so much the more as you see the Day approaching.

[10] Hebrews 10:23-25

The gathering together with other believers is not primarily designed for evangelism of unbelievers who might show up in church. We gather to "stir up love and good works" by believers, and to "exhort one another". All believers need to be part of the gathered congregation in order to grow and mature in Christ. Gathering with other believers serves to make us more effective in living out the gospel in everyday life. In Ephesians 4:11-16, Paul further explains the purpose of gathering to hear the word of God preached.

> And He Himself gave some to be apostles, some prophets, some evangelists, and some pastors and teachers, for the equipping of the saints for the work of ministry, for the edifying of the body of Christ, till we all come to the unity of the faith and of the knowledge of the Son of God, to a perfect man, to the measure of the stature of the fullness of Christ; that we should no longer be children, tossed to and fro and carried about with every wind of doctrine, by the trickery of men, in the cunning craftiness of deceitful plotting, but, speaking the truth in love, may grow up in all things into Him who is the head – Christ - from whom the whole body, joined and knit together by what every joint supplies, according to the effective working by which every part does its share, causes growth of the body for the edifying of itself in love.

Planning some evangelistic gatherings for preaching the gospel to the unsaved is good. However, in many of our churches, the Sunday morning gathering is failing in the development of mature believers. In our generation, this is the primary meeting when most of the believers are present. If the pastor is not equipping them in the faith on Sunday mornings, the believers become weak and feeble in their growth in the knowledge and experience of Jesus Christ.

Paul does recognize in his teaching about the gathered church, in 1 Corinthians 14, that an unbeliever may show up in the assembly. In verse 40, he tells the Corinthian church that they are to "do everything decently and in order." He gives specific direction that they are to give preference to 'prophecy' or preaching. Tongues-speaking is never to occur in the assembly unless there is an interpreter. While the primary focus in their gathering together was to build up one another in their faith, their worship of God, and their sharing together in the word of God would impact the unbeliever who may show up. Note 1 Corinthians 14:23-25,

> Therefore if the whole church comes together in one place, and all speak with tongues, and there come in those who are uninformed or unbelievers, will they not say that you are out of your mind?

> But if all prophesy, and an unbeliever or an uninformed person comes in, he is convinced by all, he is convicted by all. And thus the secrets of his heart are revealed; and so, falling down on his face, he will worship God and report that God is truly among you.

Paul does not advocate making the message more palatable to the unbeliever. In fact in verse twenty six, he recognizes that several may participate in the service in various ways. The important thing is that all is to be done for "edification" or building up believers; it is so "that all may learn and all may be encouraged." (Verse thirty one). Paul believed that the unbeliever would be 'convinced' and 'convicted' by the 'secrets of his heart' being revealed to him.

So let's cease playing the numbers game! Let's redefine our definition of success! Let's seek God's power and Presence! Let's refuse to be a partner to trivializing the church of Jesus Christ.

Chapter 2

The Bible: God's Revelation or Man's Ideas

The integrity, the infallibility, the reliability and the authority of God's word is foundational to true Christianity. If God's word is not absolutely true from cover to cover, we are set adrift upon a sea of uncertainty. If the Bible only contains the word of God, then we become our own judges as to what is truth from God and what is error that has been introduced by man. Many pastors and theologians today have chosen to trivialize the Bible, casting doubt upon many of its clear teachings.

Almighty God has specifically revealed Himself in the Bible. Losing confidence in the revealed, infallible and inerrant word of God leads us to trivialize God. God becomes irrelevant to us. We wonder why we are no longer experiencing the Transcendent God. When we trivialize the Bible, we have no message, no word from the Lord for our generation. Is it any wonder that we are losing the millennial generation? Drew Dyck writes this salient commentary.

> Many evangelical churches present a one-sided vision of God. We love talking about God's love, but not his holiness. We stress his immanence, but not his transcendence. How does this affect Millennials? I like the way millennial blogger Stephen Altrogge puts it in 'Untamable God'.

Why are so many young people leaving the church? I don't think it's all that complicated. God seems irrelevant to them. They see God as existing to meet their needs and make them happy. And sure, God can make them feel good, but so can a lot of other things. Making piles of money feels good. Climbing the corporate ladder feels good. Buying a motorcycle and spending days cruising around the country feels good - if God is simply one option on a buffet, why stick with God?

Millennials have a dim view of church. They are highly skeptical of religion. Yet they are still thirsty for transcendence. But when we portray God as a cosmic buddy, we lose them (they have enough friends). When we tell them that God will give them a better marriage and family, its white noise (they're delaying marriage and kids or forgoing them altogether). When we tell them they're special, we're merely echoing what educators, coaches, and parents have told them their whole lives. But when we present a ravishing vision of a loving and holy God, it just might get their attention and capture their hearts as well.[11]

The 21st century evangelical church faces similar challenges as the church at the beginning of the 20th century. Higher criticism had emerged in the latter decades of the 1800's in Europe. Many of the

---

[11] Quote from blog by Drew Dyck who is the managing editor of Leadership Journal, a Christianity Today publication for church leaders. Author of Generation Ex-Christian: Why Young Adults Are Leaving The Church...and How To Bring Them Back (Moody, 2010) and Yawning at Tigers: You Can't Tame God, So Stop Trying (Thomas Nelson, 2014).

higher critics were rationalists and naturalists. They operated from assumptions that guided their supposed findings. For example, they had already concluded that the miraculous was an impossibility. This led to the rejection of much of the Gospels because the Gospels are filled with the miraculous.

A couple of decades ago, C. S. Lewis said:

> When you turn from the New Testament to modern scholars, remember that you go among them as a sheep among wolves. Naturalistic assumptions, beggings of the question such as that which I noted on the first page of this book, will meet you on every side - even from the pens of clergymen. This does not mean (as I was once tempted to suspect) that these clergymen are disguised apostates who deliberately exploit the position and the livelihood given them by the Christian church to undermine Christianity. It comes partly from what we may call a "hangover." We all have Naturalism in our bones and even conversion does not at once work the infection out of our system. Its assumptions rush back upon the mind the moment vigilance is relaxed.
>
> . . . In using the books of such people, you must therefore be continually on guard. You must develop a nose like a bloodhound for those steps in the argument, which depend not on historical and linguistic knowledge, but on the concealed assumption that miracles are impossible, improbable, or improper.[12]

---

[12] The Best of C. S. Lewis, from his book "Miracles", (Baker Book House, Grand Rapids, Michigan) , pages 362-363

In the early 20th century, the special set of books called 'The Fundamentals: A Testimony to the Truth', generally referred to simply as 'The Fundamentals', was published. This was a set of ninety essays published from 1910 to 1915 by the Bible Institute of Los Angeles. The Fundamentals were edited by A. C. Dixon and later by Reuben Archer Torrey. The Fundamentals was first published as a twelve volume set, and later as a four volume set retaining all ninety essays. The ninety essays were written by sixty four different authors representing most of the major Protestant Christian denominations.

The essays were written to affirm conservative Protestant beliefs, especially those of the reformed tradition, and defend against ideas deemed inimical to them. They are widely considered to be the foundation of modern Christian fundamentalism.

The project was initially conceived in 1909 by California businessman Lyman Stewart and his brother Milton. They anonymously provided funds for collecting essays to set out what they believed to be the fundamentals of Christian faith, and for printing and distributing copies of the collected essays. 'The Fundamentals' was sent free to ministers, missionaries, professors of theology, YMCA and YWCA secretaries, Sunday School superintendents, and other Protestant religious workers in every English-speaking country. Over three million volumes (250,000 sets) were sent out.[13] I highly recommend this series of essays for serious study of basic biblical doctrine.

---

[13] Information about 'The Fundamentals' was obtained from the Wikipedia site on the Internet. 'The Fundamentals' can be freely downloaded from the Internet.

Many are the professed Christians who downplay, or even disdain doctrine. Doctrine refers to the primary basic teachings of Scripture and is essential for the maturation and grounding of every believer. The apostle Paul warns us of the trends that will be seen in the final days as we approach the second coming of Jesus Christ. In 2 Timothy 4:3-4, we read, "For the time will come, when they will not endure sound doctrine, but according to their own desires, because they have itching ears, they will heap for themselves teachers; and they will turn their ears away from the truth, and be turned aside to fables."

The virgin birth of Jesus Christ was one of the doctrines that was under attack from the higher critics. Rev. James Orr wrote on this subject in one of the earliest essays in 'The Fundamentals' series. Here is an excerpt from his essay.

> It is well known that the last ten or twenty years have been marked by a determined assault upon the truth of the Virgin birth of Christ. In the year 1892 a great controversy broke out in Germany, owing to the refusal of a pastor named Schrempf to use the Apostles' Creed in baptism because of dis-belief in this and other articles. Schrempf was deposed, and an agitation commenced against the doctrine of the Virgin birth which has grown in volume ever since. Other tendencies, especially the rise of an extremely radical school of historical criticism, adding force to the negative movement. The attack is not confined, indeed, to the article of the Virgin birth. It affects the whole supernatural estimate of Christ - His life, His claims, His sinlessness, His miracles, His resurrection from the dead. But the Virgin birth is assailed

with special vehemence, because it is supposed that the evidence for this miracle is more easily got rid of than the evidence for public facts, such as the resurrection. The result is that in very many quarters the Virgin birth of Christ is openly treated as a fable. Belief in it is scouted as unworthy of the twentieth century intelligence. The methods of the oldest opponents of Christianity are revived, and it is likened to the Greek and Roman stories, coarse and vile, of heroes who had gods for their fathers. A special point is made of the silence of Paul, and of the other writings of the New Testament, on this alleged wonder.

THE UNHAPPIEST FEATURE.

It is not only, however, in the circles of unbelief that the Virgin birth is discredited. In the church itself the habit is spreading of casting doubt upon the fact, or at least of regarding it as no essential part of Christian faith. This is the unhappiest feature in this unhappy controversy. Till recently no one dreamed of denying that, in the sincere profession of Christianity, this article, which has stood from the beginning in the forefront of all the great creeds of Christendom, was included. Now it is different. The truth and value of the article of the Virgin birth are challenged. The article, it is affirmed, did not belong to the earliest Christian tradition, and the evidence for it is not strong. Therefore, let it drop.

THE COMPANY IT KEEPS.

From the side of criticism, science, mythology, history and comparative religion, assault is thus made on the article long so dear to the hearts of Christians and rightly deemed by them so vital to their faith. For loud as is the voice of denial, one fact must strike every careful observer of the conflict. Among those who reject the Virgin birth of the Lord few will be found — I do not know any — who take in other respects an adequate view of the Person and work of the Savior. It is surprising how clearly the line of division here reveals itself.

My statement publicly made and printed has never been confuted, that those who accept a full doctrine of the incarnation, that is, of a true entrance of the eternal Son of God into our nature for the purposes of man's salvation - with hardly an exception accept with it the doctrine of the Virgin birth of Christ, while those who repudiate or deny this article of faith either hold a lowered view of Christ's Person, or, more commonly, reject His supernatural claims altogether. It will not be questioned, at any rate, that the great bulk of the opponents of the Virgin birth — those who are conspicuous by writing against it — are in the latter class.[14]

The evangelical church of the 21st century has been affected by the postmodern world view. The skeptical postmodern mind questions our ability to know anything for certain. Everything is relative and nothing is absolute. According to postmodern thought, absolute truth is unknowable with any degree of certainty. If you begin with the assumption that absolute truth doesn't exist, and

---

[14] The Fundamentals, Volume I, Chapter I. The Virgin Birth of Christ. By The Rev. Prof. James Orr, D. D., United Free Church College, Glasgow, Scotland.

that nothing can be known for certain, then you automatically discount the claim of Scripture to be God's revealed word. Many who claim to be evangelical have bought into this kind of thinking and have become trumpets sounding an uncertain note.

Pastors and other church leaders must unequivocally believe that the Bible is the word of God. If not, they disqualify themselves from Christian ministry. We must affirm that the Bible is a unique book, inspired by and revealing God Himself. We must believe that the message of the Bible is absolute truth given to us by God Himself.

Evangelicals have traditionally stood strong on the reliability and infallibility of the Bible. Scripture must stand as teacher and judge of all that we think and do. It both inspires and corrects our doctrine and our conduct. One's view of Scripture is pivotal and submission to its full authority is basic to the evangelical faith.

Does this kind of faith and belief in God's word mean that I have no questions about certain teachings of the Scriptures? Does my confidence in the Scriptures close my mind to difficult issues raised about the text? No, not at all! How then do I handle these questions?

Doubt or Inquiry?

Some religious leaders today tell us that doubt is good for it keeps us from naïvely accepting teachings without examination. I agree that we ought to fully examine what we are taught by others to see whether these things that we are taught are actually true and in keeping with the Bible teachings. When Paul and Silas came to Berea, they went to the Jewish synagogue where they taught the gospel of Jesus Christ. Doctor Luke, the writer of the book of Acts, commends the Bereans for their inquiring minds and their searching of the Scriptures to see whether or not the things they were hearing were true.[15] The Bereans did not doubt the Scriptures, but they believed that the Scriptures were God's word revealed to them by God Himself. They measured all that they heard from others by the standard of the Scriptures.

Every Christian ought to have an inquiring mind, seeking to understand God and his ways more fully. However this does not mean that we doubt the truth of the Bible. It does mean that we accept our humanity in our limited ability to understand God and His truth. The prophet, Isaiah, puts all of this in proper perspective, when he quotes God.

> For my thoughts are not your thoughts, nor are your ways my ways, says the Lord. For as the heavens are higher than the earth, so are my ways higher than your ways, and my thoughts than your thoughts. For as the rain comes down, and the snow from heaven, and do not return there, but water the earth, and make it bring forth and bud, that it may give seed to the sower and bread to the eater, so shall my word be that goes forth from my mouth; it shall not return unto me void, but it shall accomplish what I please, and it shall prosper in the thing for which I sent it.[16]

As human beings, we are limited in our understanding and comprehension of the omnipotent, omniscient God. We can know Him by faith with certainty. However, our comprehension

---

[15] Acts 17:11-12
[16] Isaiah 55:8-11

of Him is limited. Millard J. Erickson puts it this way:

> God is powerful as man is powerful, but much more so. When we say that God knows, we have the same meaning in mind as when we say that man knows - but while man knows something, God knows everything. God loves just as man loves, but God loves infinitely. We cannot grasp how much more of each of these qualities God possesses, or what it means to say that God has man's knowledge amplified to an infinite extent. Having observed only finite forms, we find it impossible to grasp infinite concepts. In this sense, God always remains incomprehensible. It is not that we do not have knowledge of Him, and genuine knowledge at that. Rather, the shortcoming lies in our inability to encompass Him within our knowledge. Although what we know of Him is the same as His knowledge of Himself, the degree of our knowledge is much less. It is not exhaustive knowledge of Him, as is His knowledge of Himself, and in that respect, it will be incomplete or non-exhaustive even in the eschaton. ('Eschaton' refers to the eternal kingdom of God.)[17]

I have come to believe in the God of the Bible through my faith in the gospel of Jesus Christ. According to Jesus Christ Himself, the purpose of the recorded word of God is that men might come to believe in Him, and by believing they will receive eternal life. The apostle John says, "And truly Jesus did many other signs in the presence of his disciples, which are not written in this book; but

---

[17] Christian Theology, Volume 1, Millard J. Erickson (Baker Book House, grand Rapids, Michigan), page 180

these are written, that you may believe that Jesus is the Christ, the Son of God, and that believing you may have life in His name."[18]

The resurrection of Jesus Christ has been verified by many eyewitnesses who saw Him alive, ate with Him, touched Him and spoke with Him. The apostle John begins his first epistle with this testimony about the eyewitnesses.

> That which was from the beginning, which we have heard, which we have seen with our eyes, which we have looked upon and our hands have handled, concerning the Word of life - (Word of life refers to Jesus Christ Himself) the life was manifested, and we have seen, and bear witness, and declare to you that eternal life, which was with the Father and was manifested to us - that which we have seen and heard we declare to you, that you also may have fellowship with us; and truly our fellowship is with the Father and with his Son, Jesus Christ.[19]

Some religious teachers and pastors tell us that the Gospels are unreliable because they were written years after the events of the crucifixion and the resurrection of Jesus Christ. They say that we cannot believe the Gospels, because these stories were just passed on by word of mouth from generation to generation, and recorded much later. They say that there are so many contradictions in the Gospels. Therefore how can we believe that they are true? First, the latest of the Gospels to be written was John's gospel, written sixty years after the resurrection of Jesus Christ. Secondly, through thorough   comparative   study,   the   apparent

---

[18] John 20:30-31
[19] 1 John 1:1-3

contradictions disappear and are adequately explained.

God has preserved His word. While we do not have the original manuscripts, we are confident that the Bible we possess today is almost identical with the original manuscripts. Through copious study of all the manuscripts of the New Testament that we possess today, scholars have been able to verify the original text with a substantial degree of certainty. New Testament professor Mark Strauss says the evidence indicates that the early church carefully transmitted the words and deeds of Jesus.[20] Dr. Josh McDowell reports in the year 2006, that there are now some 25,000 New Testament manuscripts, a figure that dwarfs the number of manuscripts of any other ancient book.[21] For a thorough discussion of the reliability of the Bible we now possess, I recommend to you the writings of David Limbaugh.[22]

C.S. Lewis gives this perspective as he writes in The Screwtape Letters. Remember that the Enemy is God, and the chief devil, Screwtape, is instructing a junior devil, Wormwood.

> No nation, and few individuals, are really brought into the Enemy's camp by the historical study of the biography of Jesus, simply as biography. Indeed, materials for a full biography have been withheld from men. The earliest converts were converted by a

---

[20] Mark L. Strauss, Four Portraits, One Jesus: A Survey of Jesus and the Gospels (Grand Rapids, Michigan: Zondervan, 2007), page 387

[21] Josh McDowell, Evidence for Christianity (Nashville, Tennessee: Thomas Nelson publishers, 2006), page 60

[22] David Limbaugh, Jesus on Trial (Washington, D. C., Regnery Publishing, 2014) chapters 7-10

single historical fact (the Resurrection) and a single theological doctrine (the Redemption) operating on a sense of sin which they already had - and sin, not against some new fancy-dress law produced as a novelty by a "great man," but against the old, platitudinous, universal moral law, which they had been taught by their nurses and mothers. The "Gospels" came later and were written not to make Christians, but to edify Christians already made.[23]

In the picturesque chapter of Revelation, chapter twelve, John writes concerning his vision of the struggle between the woman, who bears a special child, and a great fiery red dragon who is called the Devil and Satan. In a battle in heaven, Michael and the host of God's angels, are pitted against the great dragon and his evil angels. The great dragon Satan and his evil angels are cast out of heaven. In verse nine, we read that Satan "deceives the whole world." Satan uses many tactics in deceiving the world. One major tactic is to cause people to doubt the Bible and to drag the infallible word of God down to the status of merely good literature.

When we approach the word of God with doubts concerning its truthfulness and reliability, we fall into the same trap as Eve, as she was tempted by Satan in the Garden of Eden. Dr. Jason Lisle, Director of Research at the Institute for Creation Research, writes:

> Eve chose to evaluate the situation by her own standard. She opted to use her mind and her senses to judge who was telling the truth. She examined the tree with her eyes, and

[23] C. S. Lewis, The Best of C. S. Lewis, The Screwtape Letters (The Macmillan Company, New York, 1969), pages 82-83

recognized that it was delightful to look at, good for food, and desirable for wisdom (Genesis 3:6). Her preliminary "scientific" analysis suggested that the serpent's hypothesis might be correct and that God's Word - his clear warning - was wrong. After all, the fruit did not appear dangerous; there was nothing obviously defective with it that would suggest eating it would result in death. So, she took and ate, and gave to Adam, who did the same."

Dr. Lisle comments further: Like Eve, we are inclined to judge God's Word, based on our senses and our understanding of what is possible. For some people, God's Word passes the test, and for others it does not. But either way, the test itself is defective because it attempts to judge the infallible Word by standards that are fallible because they are human standards. We must admit that our senses can be mistaken at times (e.g., an optical illusion), and our understanding of what is possible is often wrong, as the history of science has shown. Therefore, it makes no sense to judge a perfect standard (the Word of God) by a fallible standard (human sensation and reasoning). This would be like a young child who knows nothing about mathematics going through a college-level calculus textbook and attempting to correct what he perceives to be errors.

So when Eve attempted to judge the infallible by the fallible, she was not only being immoral, but irrational as well. After all, she was attempting to use her mind and her senses to judge whether God was honest. But who made Eve's mind? God did. And who made

Eve's senses? God did. So if God were dishonest, then Eve would have no reason to trust her mind or her senses in the first place. The same is true of people today who attempt to judge the Bible by their own fallible standard . . . God expects us to reason, using our minds and to rely on our senses, but not to judge Him and His perfect Word by these lesser standards. He expects us to rely upon His revealed Word as the ultimate standard for judging everything else.[24]

Therefore, I do not doubt the truth and reliability of the Scriptures. The God, who declares that all Scripture is inspired by the Holy Spirit, used godly men to record his divine truth. He has miraculously inspired these human writers to write all that God wanted written, to write it accurately, infallibly and without error in the original manuscripts. When I am inquiring into a better understanding of a problem passage, I approach the Scriptures with confidence, without doubting their veracity and reliability. I believe God's word in its entirety, even when I have not yet reached an adequate understanding of some of its truths.

An Example for Consideration

One of the most difficult problems posed to my mind is the question of God's commanding Joshua and his armies to completely annihilate whole tribal groups, including women and children, as they were ordered to enter into the land of Canaan. To many skeptics, this issue causes them to say something like this: "I cannot believe in the God of the Old Testament who would give such a command!"

---

[24] Dr. Jason Lisle, Article entitled 'How Could Eve Know?' (Acts and Facts magazine, published by Institute for Creation Research, May, 2015) page 13

This is how I resolve this issue in my own mind. I have faith in the God of the Bible, that He is good in every way, and that He is incapable of doing any evil thing. With the patriarch Abraham, I stand confident that the Judge of all the earth will always do what is right.[25] The predominant attribute of God is His holiness. While God is also love, His love always operates under the umbrella of His holiness.

All human beings are sinners and are children of God's wrath.[26] God's holy nature cannot tolerate any sin, no matter how trivial our human minds might consider the sin to be. Revelation 20:11-15 predicts a very important coming event at the end of time; that event is known as the Great White Throne Judgment. As God is about to bring into existence the new heaven and the new earth, He will banish Satan and all of his evil angels to the lake of fire, along with all human beings whose names are not written in the Lamb's book of life. Would we accuse God of injustice, of doing evil, because He banishes all unrepentant sinners, and Satan, the instigator of our sin, to his cosmic garbage dump called hell?

The righteous and holy God revealed to us in the Bible did not overlook man's sin, nor did He excuse man's sin. Rather, God's holiness and justice demanded payment of the penalty for man's sin. God, in his great love, sent his Son, Jesus, the Christ, who became the sin sacrifice in our behalf. God's righteous holy nature was satisfied with the shed blood of the Savior. One cannot begin to understand the nature and the depth of God's love until he views the cross of Calvary from the perspective of God's divine holiness.

---

[25] Genesis 18:25
[26] Romans 3:23; 6:23; Ephesians 2:1-3

Now that we have viewed the big perspective of God's holiness and His ultimate casting of all, unrepentant, unredeemed human beings into the place of eternal punishment, let's seek to understand the command of God, to extinguish the Canaanite tribes.

Remember, Israel was under the governing hand of the holy God. The God of all the earth was governing them through Moses, revealing to them every step of their way. Joshua, who became Israel's leader upon the death of Moses, was given commands directly from God Himself. The Canaanite tribes were exceedingly wicked, worshiping idols, even to the point of sacrificing their own children to their idols.

The Scriptures show us that God had delayed His punishment of these Canaanite tribes for over 400 years before He led the Israelites into this land which He had promised to Abraham and his descendants. When God made His covenant with Abraham, in which He promised him the land of Canaan for his inheritance and his descendants' possession, He revealed to him that four generations would pass before they would receive this land. The reason for this delay was revealed to Abraham, "the iniquity of the Amorites is not yet complete."[27]

God had commanded His people that they should not intermarry and intermingle with these wicked Canaanite tribes. God was seeking a people who would follow Him completely and live as He commanded them to live. If the Israelites would spare the lives of the Canaanite peoples and allow them to live in their midst, the Israelites would be

---

[27] Genesis 15:16

inclined to become idolaters, along with the Canaanites. Mothers, who were idolaters, would raise their children to be idolaters. We see that because Israel disobeyed and did not completely destroy the Canaanite tribes, they soon adopted some of their idolatrous practices. The book of Judges tells the story of the Israelites coming under the bondage of some of these Canaanite people, all because they failed to fully occupy the land and to carry out the command of God to extinguish these Canaanite tribes from the earth.

In Genesis 6-9, we have the account of Noah and the flood. The righteous and holy God found the sinfulness of mankind deplorable and unacceptable. In one gigantic watery grave, God extinguished all of mankind with the exception of Noah and his wife, their three sons and their wives. Of all of the human race, only they found grace in the eyes of the Lord. The scriptural record tells us of the utter depravity of the human race.

> Then the LORD saw that the wickedness of man was great in the earth. And that every intent of the thoughts of his heart was only evil continually. And the LORD was sorry that He had made man on the earth, and He was grieved in His heart. So the LORD said, "I will destroy man whom I have created from the face of the earth, both man and beast, creeping thing, and birds of the air, for I am sorry that I have made them." But Noah found grace in the eyes of the LORD.[28]

In these acts of God's extensive judgment of man's sin, would you accuse God of being unrighteous

---

[28] Genesis 6:5-8

and unjust? Donald H. Madvig makes these insightful remarks on this thorny question.

> God was careful to point out that he was not arbitrarily destroying the Canaanites, just to give the land to Israel. The wickedness of the inhabitants of Canaan was the reason why God was removing them; and if Israel proved unfaithful, she too would be removed from the land (as happened in the exile) . . .

> A part of the wonderful omnipotence of God is that he works sovereignly in history to punish the wicked and to reward the righteous: "The Lord knows how to rescue godly men from trials and to hold the unrighteous for the Day of Judgment.
> (2 Peter 2:9).

> The extermination of the Canaanites is but one of the many evidences in the Bible, as well as in real life, that evil is real and that the devil exists. Evil does not flee at the snap of one's fingers. The struggle with sin and the devil took the son of God to the cross. There was no easy victory, even for him. Only by his suffering and death has he overcome evil once and for all. Those who will not be separated from their sin by repentance will be destroyed with their sin. As Jesus said, "If you do not believe that I am the one I claim to be, you will indeed die in your sin." (John, 8:24).

> God's severity in his treatment of sin and of sinners is but the obverse side of his grace and love. Sin and evil destroy the people he loves and prevent the full establishment of his glorious kingdom . . .

The most difficult thing to understand is the slaughter of innocent children. We must remember that death is not the alternate destiny of the human race, nor is it the greatest evil. Someday, God will give a full explanation, which is something that only he can do.[29]

Critics raise issues such as Jesus referring to the mustard seed as the least of all seeds. Botanists tell us there are other seeds that are smaller than the mustard seed. Was Jesus mistaken? Did Jesus not know about seeds; after all He is the Creator of all things. Some explain that in the context of Israel, the mustard seed was the smallest seed known to His audience. The point that Jesus is making in the parable is that this very smallest of seeds grows into a large plant, providing shelter and a home for the birds of the air. This is how the kingdom of heaven grows![30]

To the honest believing seeker, such explanations are helpful even though they may not completely satisfy our human intellect. However, to the unbelieving skeptic, nothing is satisfactory. Why? Most unbelieving skeptics are not seeking for further understanding in order that they might believe. Most unbelieving skeptics are seeking to justify their rejection of God and to avoid their accountability to God. When the heart is rebellious toward its Creator, it desires darkness rather than light because its deeds are evil.[31]

---

[29] Donald H. Madvig, commentary on Joshua, (The Expositor's Bible Commentary, Volume 3, Zondervan Publishing House, Grand Rapids, Michigan, 1992), page 247
[30] Matthew 13:31-32
[31] John 3:19

Science and the Bible

The Bible is not a science textbook and God did not intend it to be. However, the Bible never contradicts proven science. It is not my purpose to delve into all the intricacies of the creation-evolution debate.[32] It is simply true, however, that many scientists have gone far beyond the field of science when they proclaim that everything came into existence billions of years ago through the process of evolution. To the scientists who assert this kind of dogmatic statement, I simply ask, "Were you there when God created the heavens and the earth by His spoken word?[33]

The theory that the earth is billions of years old is based upon assumptions of uniformitarianism and upon several different methods of testing the age of the earth. Many reputable scientists have questioned the reliability of these testing methods. Have all things been uniform since the beginning of time? No! Whenever a catastrophe happens uniformity goes out the window. Therefore, I choose to believe what the Bible says, and wait for science to catch up with the Bible.

Some scientists jumped on the bandwagon when one of their colleagues stated that there is a possibility of a self-creating universe. This is, of course, is not science but contradictory nonsense. Someone has wisely said, "Scientists have discovered that people will believe anything if you claim that scientists have discovered it."

---

[32] The Institute for Creation Research has many true scientists, who believe in God and the Bible, are doing great research and producing great materials supporting biblical truth. They hold the position of a young earth.
[33] Genesis 1

There are some laws that are built into nature by God himself that are irrefutable. Gravity, for example, is a force that pulls everything toward the center of our planet. Science has discovered that when you get a certain distance above our earth, gravity no longer has an effect upon you. If it was not for the force of gravity created by God, everything would float around at random and our world would be chaos.

Scientific method is based on observation that leads to a theory or explanation of facts that is consistent with what has been observed. That theory or explanation is then tested in every way possible to see whether or not it is true. True science will never contradict the Bible nor will the Bible contradict true science. The problem is that much that is called science is not true science. Much of what is called science is really nothing more than the speculations and unproven theories of one who claims to be a scientist. Many scientists who do not believe in God are seeking for explanations of the existence of all things apart from an Intelligent Creator.

Ravi Zacharias shares this about Malcom Muggeridge, a British journalist, who most of his life was an unbelieving skeptic. Muggeridge wrote to Mother Theresa and told her he had no interest in Christianity because of all its duplicity. Mother Theresa responded, "Your problem is a finite one. God is infinite. Let the infinite take care of your finite struggle." That caused Muggeridge to bow his knee to Christ and he called it the most fulfilling step he had ever taken in his life. In a similar way, my faith is in the Eternal God, the intelligent Creator of all things. True science is nothing more nor less than the discovery of what God created and put in motion. The word of God is true in its entirety and true science will never be contrary to what God's word declares.

The Uniqueness of the Bible

Here some facts about the Bible. It is one volume made up of sixty six different books. God, the author, has used over forty different men to write down His message to us over a period of sixteen hundred years. The Bible displays consistent unity throughout its pages, even though it was written over this lengthy period of time by many different authors. The Bible has proven to be historically accurate in its reference to people, places and events. Josh McDowell says,

> The science of archaeology and secular historical records have repeatedly confirmed the precision of the references in various biblical books. The minute attention to detail observed by biblical writers is unparalleled in any other ancient literature.[34]

The Bible is scientifically accurate. Although the Bible is not primarily intended to be a scientific textbook, wherever it does speak of scientific matters, it has proven to be accurate.

The Bible's Own Claims

Bible itself claims to be the very word of God, uniquely inspired by the Holy Spirit of God. 2 Peter 1:20-21 says, ". . . knowing this first, that no prophecy of Scripture is of any private interpretation, for prophecy never came by the will of man, but holy men of God spoke as they were

---

[34] Josh McDowell, Five Tough Questions (Tyndale House Publishers, Wheaton, Illinois, 1991), page 7

moved by the Holy Spirit." 2 Timothy 3:16 states unequivocally, "All scripture is given by inspiration of God."

The psalmist, in Psalm 119, declares his absolute confidence in the Word of God. Almost every verse of the one hundred seventy six verses in this Psalm speaks of the word of God, referring to the word of God as God's statutes, God's commandments, God's precepts, God's law, God's judgments and God's word. Here are just a few verses that demonstrate how the psalmist revered and trusted the eternal Word of God.

> Psalm 119:89: "Forever, O Lord, your word is settled in heaven."

> Psalm 119:93: "I will never forget your precepts, for by them You have given me life."

> Psalm 119:104 - 105: "Through your precepts I get understanding; Therefore, I hate every false way. Your word is a lamp to my feet and a light to my path."

> Psalm 119:128: "Therefore all your precepts concerning all things I consider to be right; I hate every false way."

Christ Jesus Himself affirmed the truthfulness of God's word. Matthew 5:17-18 records the words of Jesus, as He gives us His very high view of Scripture: "Do not think that I came to destroy the Law, or the Prophets. I did not come to destroy but to fulfill. For assuredly, I say to you, till heaven and earth pass away, one jot or one tittle will by no means pass from the law till all is fulfilled." Jesus also claimed that the very words He spoke were given Him by God the Father, and, in the last day, the Day of Judgment, His words would judge unbelievers who reject Him.[35]

The Bible claims the absolute authority of God. God promises that His word is powerful and accomplishes God's purpose. It will convict sinners by shining God's holy light into their hearts. The apostle Paul said that "faith comes by hearing, and hearing by the word of God."[36] It is the word of God that will lead the believer to maturity in Jesus Christ. The apostle Paul also said that the inspired Scriptures are "profitable for doctrine, for reproof, for correction, for instruction in righteousness that the man of God may be complete, thoroughly equipped for every good work."[37]

The prophet Jeremiah gives this command from God: "He who has my word, let him speak my word faithfully. What is the chaff to the wheat?" says the LORD, "And is not my word like a fire?" says the LORD, "and like a hammer that breaks the rock into pieces?"[38]

Hebrews 4:12 says, "For the word of God is living and active, sharper than any double-edged sword; it penetrates even to dividing soul and spirit, joints and marrow; it judges the thoughts and attitudes of the heart."

Dr. Henry M. Morris III says, "It is still true that many churches are trying to strike the right balance between modern expectations and genuine worship. It is also true that most pastors are trying their best to teach and

---

[35] John 12:47-50
[36] Romans 10:17
[37] 2 Timothy 3:16-17
[38] Jeremiah 23:28-29

preach God's Word. Some congregations, however, tend to reward non-controversy over a clear stand on God's Word. Some are caught up in petty disputes that drive those who are hungry and thirsting after righteousness back into the godless world - or worse yet, hardened their hearts against the 'living word' that could free them. Perhaps the sounds of the world are drowning out the message of God. Perhaps the 'renewing of our mind' is held back from 'transforming' our lives (Romans 12:1-2) because the heart is beating too loudly with the 'lust of the flesh' (1 John 2:16).

This is not a new problem among the churches. Among the seven churches to the Lord Jesus addressed himself in the early chapters of the book of Revelation, there were only two (Philadelphia and Smyrna) that were not reprimanded for some serious difficulty. Two (Ephesus and Laodicea) were warned that they were even in danger of losing their very "churchness" (lose its authority as a church, have its lampstand removed). Those seven churches, representative of all churches since our Lord returned to His throne, set the stage - both good and bad - for what we should pay attention to."[39]

True Wisdom Grounded Eternally In God

In 2 Timothy 3:15 the apostle Paul encouraged Timothy to continue on in the things that he had

---

[39] Dr. Henry M. Morris III, Article: Sounds of Music, Words of Truth (Acts & Facts magazine, published by Institute for Creation Research, Dallas, Texas) August 2015, page 6

been taught from childhood for the Holy Scriptures "are able to make you wise for salvation through faith which is in Christ Jesus." Salvation is more than the initial acceptance of Christ and His atoning work on the cross as one's passage into eternal life as a free gift. Salvation is the process of transformation that continues as a person submits to growing to be more like Christ.

King Solomon met God in a dream one night shortly after being anointed as king. God said to him, "Ask! What shall I give you?" He requested an "understanding heart to judge Your people, that I may discern between good and evil." God granted his request and Solomon was regarded as a very wise and discerning king.[40]

In Proverbs 8 Solomon personifies wisdom and presents godly wisdom as the most desirable of all treasures. Wisdom is tied to the very eternal nature of God Himself before anything was created by God.

> The LORD possessed me (wisdom) at the beginning of His way, before His works of old. I have been established from everlasting, from the beginning, before there was ever an earth.
>
> When there were no depths, I was brought forth, when there no fountains abounding with water. Before the mountains were settled, before the hills, I was brought forth. While as yet He had not made the earth or the fields, or the primal dust of the world.

---

[40] 1 Kings 3:5ff

When He prepared the heavens, I was there, when He drew a circle on the face of the deep, when He established the clouds above, when He strengthened the fountains of the deep, when He assigned to the sea its limit, so that the waters would not transgress His command, when He marked out the foundations of the earth, then I was beside Him as a master craftsman, and I was daily His delight, rejoicing always before Him, rejoicing in His inhabited world, and my delight was with the sons of men.[41]

The Scriptures contrast godly eternal wisdom and worldly wisdom. Godly wisdom leads us to know the truth and to seek to walk in the truth of God. Worldly wisdom leads to pride, to bitter envy and self-seeking. This wisdom is "earthly, sensual, and demonic." Godly wisdom, or wisdom from above, "is first pure, then peaceable, gentle, willing to yield, full of mercy and good fruits . . ."[42]

There is no eternal wisdom apart from God. Therefore James exhorts us, "If any man lack wisdom, let him ask of God, who gives to all liberally and without reproach, and it will be given unto him."[43] The primary source of that wisdom is the Bible, the eternal word of God.

In this age of uncertainty we must reaffirm our confidence in the word of God. Believe it in its entirety and stand firmly upon it. Preach it and teach it passionately as the Oracle of God.

---

[41] Proverbs 8:22-31
[42] James 3:13-18
[43] James 1:5

Chapter 3

It Is All About Jesus Christ

Who is Jesus Christ? That is the most crucial question. Is He God? Or is He simply a good man, a wonderful philosopher and a great teacher? You must decide! Is He really who He claimed to be? If not, then He is not a good man or a worthy teacher. He then is an imposter leading people astray and down a pathway that leads to nowhere. C. S. Lewis says,

> I am trying here to prevent anyone saying the really foolish thing that people often say about Him: I'm ready to accept Jesus as a great moral teacher, but I don't accept his claim to be God. That is the one thing we must not say. A man who was merely a man and said the sort of things Jesus said would not be a great moral teacher. He would either be a lunatic - on the level with the man who says he is a poached egg - or else he would be the Devil of Hell. You must make your choice. Either this man was, and is, the Son of God, or else a madman or something worse. You can shut him up for a fool, you can spit at him and kill him as a demon or you can fall at his feet and call him Lord and God, but let us not come with any patronizing nonsense about his being a great human teacher. He has not left that open to us. He did not intend to . . . Now it seems to me obvious that He was neither a lunatic nor a fiend: and consequently, however strange or terrifying or

unlikely it may seem, I have to accept the view that He was and is God. [44]

Does your church exalt and magnify Jesus Christ as the God-Man? Do you as a pastor or church leader regard Him as the unique Son of God? Every time you preach, do you hold Him up before the flock over which the Lord has made you overseer?

Paul, the apostle, writing to the Corinthian church, said, "Therefore, from now on, we regard no one according to the flesh. Even though we have known Christ according to the flesh, yet now we know Him thus no longer."[45] While Christ walked this earth, many people regarded Him as merely a human being, albeit a very wise and capable human being. Paul himself, before his experience of confrontation by Christ on the Damascus Road, thought of Christ as only a human being who was blaspheming God by His claims. After meeting the risen Christ, his whole viewpoint of who Jesus Christ is, was completely transformed.

Paul proclaims that anyone who believes in Christ, or who is 'in Christ' is a new creation, not simply a natural human being.[46] Jesus Christ transforms the truly repentant believer and reconciles him with the heavenly Father.

In many of our churches, we are trivializing Jesus as if He was simply one of us, very much like us, and that He is merely a human being? Our culture often will refer to Jesus Christ in a flippant way by referring to him as 'the man upstairs', or they will

---

[44] C.S. Lewis, Mere Christianity, (London: Collins, 1952), pages 54 – 56. (In all editions, this is Bk. II, Ch. 3, "The Shocking Alternative
[45] 2 Corinthians 5:16
[46] 2 Corinthians 5:17

refer to God as 'the big guy in the sky'. When we as believers refer to Jesus and the heavenly Father in this flippant way, we dishonor our Savior and God.

It is true that Jesus Christ became flesh and is one hundred percent human. By His incarnation (God becoming man), He bridged the gulf between God and man. However, He is also one hundred percent Deity. He is the God-Man! While Jesus Christ has opened the way to the Father and we are invited to enter into His presence without fear of rejection, nevertheless we must treat Him with reverence and awe.

Every pastor who considers himself to be an evangelical would readily say that he believes Jesus Christ is God. However, it is a good exercise to frequently analyze what is happening in your church. Is Jesus Christ always foremost and in the forefront of the ministries of the church? Is He exalted and glorified by all that we do? Could a person enter your church worship services and leave without experiencing the presence and the power of our Lord Jesus Christ? Would that person know that it is all about Jesus Christ? Would he go away from your church saying, "What a great and wonderful Savior is Jesus Christ?"

What the Bible Says About the Identity of Jesus Christ?

The apostle John refers to Jesus Christ as "His only begotten Son".[47] This is the translation of the Greek word 'monogenes' which means 'the only one of His kind'. Therefore, some translations have used the word 'unique'. Jesus Christ is the unique One who has come from the heavenly Father. Jesus

---

[47] John 1:14, 3:16

Christ is the eternal Son of God, who took on human flesh in order to bridge the great chasm between the holy God and sinful man. There has never been, nor ever will be, anyone like Him! Jesus Christ stands alone; He is incomparable!

In John 1:14 John, the apostle, declares, "And the Word (Jesus Christ) became flesh and dwelt among us, and we beheld His glory, the glory as of the only begotten of the Father, full of grace and truth."

What did John mean when he said, "we beheld His glory?"

An elderly retired pastor, Ray, who was in an assisted-living home, defined 'glory' as "excellence on exhibition." I would simply add, "God's excellence and majesty on display or on exhibition."

As we study the Gospels, we find many references to the disciples and the crowds being awestruck or overcome by the words and the actions of Jesus Christ. When Jesus was twelve years of age, He was answering questions of the rabbis in the temple. Luke observes, "All who heard him were astonished at His understanding and answers." [48]

As Jesus concluded His teaching of the 'Sermon on the Mount' Matthew tells us that "the people were astonished at His teaching, for He taught them, as one having authority, and not as the scribes."[49] As Jesus Christ healed the paralytic, Mark's gospel tells us the reaction of the crowd. "All were amazed and glorified God, saying, "We never saw anything like this!"[50]

---

[48] Luke 2:47
[49] Matthew 7:28, 29
[50] Mark 2:12

Luke records the incident when Jesus took Peter, James and John up a mountain to pray. While he was praying, Peter, James and John were "heavy with sleep." When they were fully awake, they witnessed the transfiguration of Jesus; the "appearance of his face was altered, and his robe became white and glistening . . ." Two men, Moses and Elijah talked with Jesus. Luke tells us that they "appeared in glory and spoke of His decease which He was about to accomplish at Jerusalem."[51]

Jesus performed miracle after miracle before the disciples and the people of Israel. On more than one occasion Jesus calmed the storms on the Sea of Galilee when the disciples were convinced that they would perish in the waves. A typical response of the disciples was "so the men marveled, saying, "Who can this be, that even the winds and the sea obey Him?"[52]

The response to Jesus' glory was either worship or unbelief and opposition. Many of the scribes and the Pharisees, the priests and the religious leaders, sought to quiet Jesus by plotting his death. Even at the time of His trial and His death on the cross, some marveled and came to believe that He indeed is the Son of God. One of the criminals crucified alongside Jesus blasphemed Him and died in his sin. The other criminal, a thief, cried out for mercy and Jesus assured him "today you will be with Me in Paradise".[53]

Following the glorious appearance of the risen Christ, Luke tells of two men who were walking to the village of Emmaus. Jesus joins them in their journey, asking them about their conversation along

---

[51] Luke 9:28-36
[52] Matthew 8:27
[53] Luke 23:39-43

the way. Cleopas, one of the two, answered Jesus, "Are you the only stranger in Jerusalem, and have you not known the things which happened there in these days?" Jesus invites Cleopas to tell Him of the events that he had observed. Jesus then responded, "Ought not the Christ to have suffered these things and to enter into His glory?" Beginning at Moses and all the prophets, Jesus, "expounded to them in all the Scriptures the things concerning Himself." Jesus, at their invitation, stayed with them that evening. Luke tells us that Jesus sat at the table with them.

> He took bread, blessed and broke it, and gave it to them. Then their eyes were opened, and they knew Him; and He vanished from their sight. And they said to one another, "Did not our heart burn within us while He talked with us on the road, and while He opened the Scriptures to us?[54]

The apostle John wrote his gospel account for one stated purpose. In John 20:30-31, John states the purpose of his writing.

> And truly Jesus did many other signs in the presence of His disciples, which are not written in this book; but these are written, that you may believe that Jesus is the Christ, the Son of God, and that believing you may have life in His name.

Throughout his gospel account John records many "I am" declarations of Jesus. Jesus said, "I am the bread of life;"[55] "I am the light of the world;"[56] "I

---

[54] Read Luke 24:13-35
[55] John 6:35, 48, 51
[56] John 8:12

am the door;"[57] "I am the good shepherd;"[58] "I am the resurrection and the life;"[59] "I am the way, the truth, and the life;"[60] "I am the true vine."[61]

Each and every time that Jesus made the statement, "I AM", He openly declared himself as Jehovah God. As Jesus was teaching in the temple, He emphasized repeatedly that He was from the heavenly Father, from above and sent from God Himself. Many of the Jews believed in Him and many others rejected Him, claiming that they were sons and daughters of Abraham.

Jesus could not have declared His Deity more clearly when He said, "Your father Abraham rejoiced to see My day, and he saw it and was glad." Then the Jews said to Him, "You are not yet fifty years old, and have you seen Abraham?" Jesus replied to them unequivocally, "Most assuredly, I say to you, before Abraham was, I AM."[62]

Jesus was crystal clear in His claim. The unbelieving Jews understood Jesus claims to be Jehovah God who had appeared to Moses as he was tending the sheep of his father-in-law, Jethro. This is the reason that the Jews took up stones and sought to kill Him. When God appeared to Moses in the bush that was burning but was not consumed by the flames, God said to Moses, "I am the God of your father-the God of Abraham, the God of Isaac, and the God of Jacob." When Moses questioned whom he would say had sent him to the enslaved

---

[57] John 10:7, 9
[58] John 10:11, 14
[59] John 11:25
[60] John 14:6
[61] John 15:1, 5
[62] John 8:56-58

people of Israel, God replied, "I AM WHO I AM."[63]

Jesus Christ is the wonderful and exalted Savior. He is the pivot point of history. He is the Lamb of God and the Lion of Judah. John the Baptist introduced Him as the Lamb of God who takes away the sin of the world. John, the apostle, confirmed it in his gospel and in the book of Revelation. The book of Revelation calls Him 'the Lamb of God' at least twenty times.

Jesus Christ is the only Savior, the Lamb of God, who takes away the sin of the world. He is Alpha and Omega, the beginning and the end. He is 'I AM WHO I AM', the Lord of lords and King of kings.

The Second Coming of Jesus Christ

The second coming of Jesus Christ is neglected in the preaching and teaching of many churches today. Almost all of the churches make much of the birth of Jesus Christ. Because we have a specially designated time on our calendar when we celebrate Christmas, the first coming of Jesus is prominently taught and preached. Many sermons will be preached on the virgin birth and the fulfillment of prophecies of the Old Testament through the birth of Jesus at Bethlehem. Many sermons will emphasize the redemptive reason for the incarnation of Christ Jesus.

We celebrate the death, burial and resurrection of Jesus Christ at another calendar event usually called Good Friday and Easter Sunday. At least at this time of the year, there is much emphasis upon the

---

[63] Exodus 3:6, 13-14

reason for Jesus Christ's first coming to our planet. Sermons abound on the substitutionary death of Jesus on the cross; there is much preaching concerning the reality and significance of the resurrection of Jesus Christ.

The contrast is amazing! In many of our 21st century western-world churches, the second coming of Jesus Christ receives very little attention. In some churches, as you analyze the preaching over several years, you will find not one single sermon on the subject of the second coming of Jesus Christ.

The Bible presents God's work of redemption as an ongoing process which reaches its final climax when Christ returns the second time to restore His creation to its original perfection. The final phase of the process of redemption began with the first coming of Jesus when He came, for the purpose of dying a substitutionary death for the sins of mankind. During His first coming He rose from the dead as the victor over Satan, sin, death and hell. In the events of His second coming, Jesus Christ will come to this earth to begin the final process establishing His rule of righteousness in His eternal kingdom.

In Acts 1, we find the account of His ascension into heaven to the right hand of the Heavenly Father. As Jesus ascended, two men dressed in white apparel (probably two angels appearing as men) clearly promised that He would return in like manner as they witnessed Him ascending into heaven.[64] The work of redemption will culminate in the events surrounding His Second Coming. There will be a final judgment of all people, both the living and the dead. The true believers will receive new immortal

---

[64] Acts 1:9-11

bodies for eternal life; the wicked will be cast into hell. There will be a final defeat and destruction of all evil - Satan, sin, suffering and death. The kingdom of God will come to its fulfillment at last.

While there is much debate about the details of His second coming, there can be no doubt that His second coming will come to pass. Some distinguish between two phases of His second coming, the rapture of believers and the second coming of Jesus Christ to judge the world. Others interpret the second coming as two phases of one event.

Many pastors today avoid the subject of prophecy, including the clear teaching of the second coming of Jesus Christ. One reason may be because of the dogmatism of some preachers who project every detail of their particular interpretation of coming events as the only correct view. Another reason may be because of the date setting by some foolish preachers who ignore the teachings of Jesus, when he said: "But of that day and hour no one knows, not even the angels of heaven, but my Father only."[65]

It is not my purpose to debate pre-millennialism, post-millennialism, or a-millennialism. Whatever eschatological system of interpretation you hold, there are some basic teachings regarding the end times that are clear in Scripture. Let the clear teachings of Scripture influence your eschatological system rather than the reverse.

• Jesus Christ will appear on this earth a second time, coming in a manner similar to His ascension into heaven.[66]

---

[65] Matthew 24:36
[66] Acts 1:9-11; Hebrews 9:27-28

• Jesus Christ promises a prepared place for every prepared person who comes to the prepared way, Jesus Christ Himself.[67] He will come to receive us to Himself, so that we will be with Him forever. This blessed hope is presented in Scripture as a great incentive and motivation for holy living and obedience to Jesus Christ, our Savior and Lord.

• The born-again believer is promised resurrection to an immortal body which will no longer be subject to disease or sorrow of any kind. Believers who have died will be raised first, then those who are alive at His coming for His redeemed people will be raised, and we will meet the Lord in the air. So shall we ever be with the Lord![68]

• Jesus Christ also has promised to return to the earth, coming in great glory and witnessed by all inhabitants of the earth.[69] Both Old and New Testaments predict a terrible time of trouble that will precede this coming of Christ to the earth. During this Great Tribulation a great evil ruler called Antichrist will emerge as a world ruler. He will oppose God in every way and will demand exclusive worship. Jesus Christ will return to the earth and destroy these enemies of God.[70]

• National Israel has been scattered amongst the nations for almost two millennia. God's word predicted this scattering amongst the nations because of their rebellion against God. God's word also predicted that someday God would gather them back to their own land from amongst the nations. National Israel came back into existence in 1948. Those who believe in replacement theology ought

---

[67] John 14:1-6
[68] 1 Thessalonians 4:13-18; 1 Corinthians 15:50-58
[69] Matthew 24:29-31
[70] 2 Thessalonians 2:1-12; Daniel 9; Book of Revelation, etc.

to reconsider their theological position.[71] The existence of the nation of Israel contradicts this interpretation of Scripture and confirms the statement of the apostle Paul in Romans 11:1. "I say, then, has God cast away His people? Certainly not!"

• At the end of the Great Tribulation, many nations of the world, led by the Antichrist, will gather to seek to defeat Israel. Jesus Christ will act in behalf of Israel and the armies of the world's nations will be defeated. We already see many enemy nations surrounding Israel who have the obliteration of the nation of Israel as their goal. However, God will defend His people, fight for them and bring justice in their behalf.[72]

• The Scriptures teach that Jesus Christ will establish His reign over all the earth for one thousand years. Revelation 20:1-3 tells us that an angel from heaven will chain Satan and cast him into the bottomless pit where he will be bound for a millennium. He will have no power to deceive the nations until the thousand years are over. Verse four says that those who were "beheaded for their witness to Jesus and for the word of God, who had not worshiped the beast or his image, and had not received his mark on their foreheads or on their hands" will "live and reign with Christ for a thousand years." The prophet Isaiah foretells this time of peace and prosperity where "the wolf and the lamb shall feed together, the lion shall eat straw like the ox, and dust shall be the serpent's food.

---

[71] Replacement theology is the belief that Israel has been replaced by the church. This system believes that the promises made to Israel now belong to the church. It also teaches that God is finished with national Israel.
[72] Revelation 19:11-21

They shall not hurt nor destroy in all My holy mountain, says the Lord."[73]

• Following the millennial reign of Jesus Christ on the earth, Satan will be released for a time, and will go out once again to deceive the nations. He will lead them in opposition to Christ Jesus, despite the fact that they have experienced prosperity and peace under His reign. In this final battle of Gog and Magog, Satan and his followers will be defeated by God Almighty. Fire will come down from God and consume the numerous hosts of the army of Satan.[74] This will be the final end of Satan as he will be cast into the lake of fire with the beast and the false prophet.

• The Great White Throne Judgment will then take place where all non-believers of all time will appear before God for final judgment. They will be judged 'guilty', according to their works which are recorded in God's books. Another book, the 'Book of Life', will be checked and if their names are not found written in the pages of that book they will be cast into the lake of fire.[75]

• Revelation 21 and 22 tells us there will be the new heaven and the new earth. This is the final eternal abode of the saved, those who are righteous, not through their own works, but through the righteousness of Jesus Christ granted to them because of their repentance and faith in Jesus Christ. All human beings who will dwell in the new heaven and the new earth are there because of the grace of the Lord Jesus Christ. The old earth will

---

[73] Isaiah 65:25
[74] Revelation 20:7-10
[75] Revelation 20:11-15

pass away, consumed by fire, as the elements melt with fervent heat.[76]

Pastor, don't neglect prophecy just because it is difficult and sometimes controversial. Share the clear truths of prophecy with boldness and confidence. Avoid going beyond what the Scriptures clearly teach. If you speculate, make certain you are not doing it to be sensational, and let the people know that this speculation is simply your own ideas. Do not project dates but let your people know that the end is nearer than when they first believed. Urge them with all fervency to live holy lives, in the midst of a darkening and passing world.

> Therefore, since all these things will be dissolved, what manner of persons ought you to be in holy conduct and godliness, looking for and hastening the coming of the day of God, because of which the heavens will be dissolved, being on fire, and the elements will melt with fervent heat?
>
> Nevertheless we, according to His promise, look for new heavens and a new earth in which righteousness dwells. Therefore, beloved, looking forward to these things, be diligent to be found in Him in peace, without spot and blameless.
>
> You, therefore, beloved, since you know this beforehand, beware lest you also fall from your own steadfastness, being led away with the error of the wicked; but grow in the grace and knowledge of our Lord and Savior Jesus Christ. To Him be glory both now and forever. Amen.[77]

---

[76] 2 Peter 3:10
[77] 2 Peter 3:11-14; 17-18

Worship Him and Exalt Him

As the song writer Robert Cull wrote in this wonderful worship chorus, "Open our eyes, Lord; I want to see Jesus. To reach out and touch Him, to show Him I love Him. Open my ears, Lord, and help me to listen. Open my eyes, Lord, I want to see Jesus."

Is your church holding up Jesus Christ in a true and meaningful way? When we gather together as the Lord's redeemed people, we should be brought face to face once again with our wonderful Lord Jesus. Is your church one that trivializes Jesus by neglect? Do your worship leaders exalt Jesus Christ and lift Him up on high? Does your pastor preach Christ and Him crucified and risen again from the dead, coming again and alive forevermore? Does your congregation leave with a determination to live godly lives as they are "looking for the blessed hope and glorious appearing of our great God and Savior Jesus Christ, who gave Himself for us, that He might redeem us from every lawless deed and purify for Himself His own special people, zealous for good works?"[78]

The goal of each church must be to practice the words of John, the Baptist, "He must increase, but I must decrease!"[79]

The late Dr. S. M. Lockridge, a pastor from San Diego, California certainly exalted Jesus Christ when he spoke these inspiring words concluding a

---

[78] Titus 2:13, 14
[79] John 3:30

sermon entitled "That's My King", given in Detroit in 1976.[80]

My King was born King. The Bible says He's a Seven Way King. He's the King of the Jews - that's an Ethnic King. He's the King of Israel - that's a National King. He's the King of righteousness. He's the King of the ages. He's the King of Heaven. He's the King of glory. He's the King of kings and He is the Lord of lords. Now that's my King.

Well, I wonder if you know Him. Do you know Him? Don't try to mislead me. Do you know my King? David said the Heavens declare the glory of God, and the firmament shows His handiwork. My King is the only one of whom there are no means of measure that can define His limitless love. No far seeing telescope can bring into visibility the coastline of the shore of His supplies. No barriers can hinder Him from pouring out His blessing.

He's enduringly strong. He's entirely sincere. He's eternally steadfast. He's immortally graceful. He's imperially powerful. He's impartially merciful. That's my King. He's God's Son. He's the sinner's Savior. He's the centerpiece of civilization. He stands alone in Himself. He's honest. He's unique. He's unparalleled. He's unprecedented. He's supreme. He's pre-eminent. He's the grandest idea in literature. He's the highest personality in philosophy. He's the supreme problem in higher criticism. He's the fundamental

[80] http://www.rpmministries.org/2009/12/thats-my-king-do-you-know-him/

doctrine of historic theology. He's the carnal necessity of spiritual religion. That's my King.

He's the miracle of the age. He's the superlative of everything good that you choose to call Him. He's the only one able to supply all our needs simultaneously. He supplies strength for the weak. He's available for the tempted and the tried. He sympathizes and He saves. He's the Almighty God who guides and keeps all his people. He heals the sick. He cleanses the lepers. He forgives sinners. He discharges debtors. He delivers the captives. He defends the feeble. He blesses the young. He serves the unfortunate. He regards the aged. He rewards the diligent and He beautifies the meek. That's my King.

Do you know Him? Well, my King is a King of knowledge. He's the wellspring of wisdom. He's the doorway of deliverance. He's the pathway of peace. He's the roadway of righteousness. He's the highway of holiness. He's the gateway of glory. He's the master of the mighty. He's the captain of the conquerors. He's the head of the heroes. He's the leader of the legislatures. He's the overseer of the overcomers. He's the governor of governors. He's the Prince of princes. He's the King of kings and He's the Lord of lords. That's my King.

His office is manifold. His promise is sure. His light is matchless. His goodness is limitless. His mercy is everlasting. His love never changes. His Word is enough. His grace is sufficient. His reign is righteous. His yoke is easy and His burden is light. I wish I could describe Him to you but He's indescribable.

That's my King. He's incomprehensible, He's invincible, and He is irresistible.

I'm coming to tell you that the heavens of heavens can't contain Him, let alone some man explain Him. You can't get Him out of your mind. You can't get Him off of your hands. You can't outlive Him and you can't live without Him. The Pharisees couldn't stand Him, but they found out they couldn't stop Him. Pilate couldn't find any fault in Him. The witnesses couldn't get their testimonies to agree about Him. Herod couldn't kill Him. Death couldn't handle Him and the grave couldn't hold Him. That's my King.

He always has been and He always will be. I'm talking about the fact that He had no predecessor and He'll have no successor. There's nobody before Him and there'll be nobody after Him. You can't impeach Him and He's not going to resign. That's my King! That's my King!

Thine is the kingdom and the power and the glory. Well, all the power belongs to my King. We're around here talking about black power and white power and green power, but in the end all that matters is God's power. Thine is the power. Yeah. And the glory. We try to get prestige and honor and glory for ourselves, but the glory is all His. Yes. Thine is the Kingdom and the power and glory, forever and ever and ever and ever. How long is that? Forever and ever and ever and ever. . . And when you get through with all of the 'evers', then . . . Amen!

Chapter 4

Worship or Entertainment

On a recent visit to one of the campuses of a three-campus mega-church, I experienced what I fear is occurring frequently in our evangelical churches across the Western world. We were greeted by very friendly hosts and hostesses at the welcome center. They were smiling, gracious and made us feel very welcome. Before we entered the worship center, they offered us earplugs if we so desired.

Upon entering the worship center, we chose to sit near the back. The worship center, we were told by an older person seated nearby, could accommodate about 1300 people. I estimated that about three hundred to three hundred fifty had assembled by the time the service began. Theater lighting illuminated the platform area. On the large projection screen, a clock was ticking down to the start time. Precisely when the clock ticked down to zero, the worship team began to lead in 'worship music'. The lead worship person, playing an electric guitar, was backed up by several other guitars and a drum set.

It was contemporary rock style music. We were not familiar with any of the songs that they played and sang. The volume was so loud that the whole building was shaking. We could not understand any of the words that were being sung. As we looked around to observe the congregation we could only see perhaps a half dozen people who were singing. We felt like we were at a rock concert, with a rock band upfront performing.

Being an older man from another generation, admittedly contemporary music is not my favorite style. But this is not about contemporary versus traditional music. Certainly music varies in different cultures and different times. It is about the issue of entertainment verses true worship. This was obviously entertainment, designed to attract a crowd, performed by some frustrated 'musicians' who had found their place to perform.

We might have been able to endure this experience had it not been for what followed. The pastor appeared on the platform following the rock band. The very first words out of his mouth were "are you having fun today?" This was when my wife and I decided to leave. As we were making our exit, an older lady pursued us and ask if we were leaving. I responded, "Yes, I do not think this is for us!" As we walked to our car, we passed the welcome center and the greeters were still there. Two older ladies and an older gentleman spoke to us saying, "You're going the wrong direction!" When I told them that we were leaving, they asked "Why?" So I tried graciously as possible to explain why.

I told them that we were very disappointed by our experience. First of all, the music was so loud that even I, who suffers from some hearing loss already, found it very uncomfortable. The decibel level was so high that it was hurting our ears. However, when the pastor's first words were "are you having fun today?" we felt it was time to leave. I continued to explain to them that our understanding of worship was not primarily that we would have fun.

C.S. Lewis wrote, "I didn't go to religion to make me happy. I always knew a bottle of Port would do that. If you want a religion to make you feel really comfortable, I certainly don't recommend Christianity."

We are continuing to adapt to the culture around us rather than challenging our culture with the truth of God's word. We did not come to have fun; we had come to seriously worship our great God and our wonderful Savior. It was sad to find that all three of them agreed with me. They said, "We don't like it either."

I wondered, as we drove away, "Why do they stay?" Maybe it is because they cannot find a church in their community that is not going the same direction. Perhaps they do not want to be seen as critical or negative. Or this church has been their church for decades and they do not want to abandon it.

Often people who oppose these changes in evangelical churches are told that they just don't like change. They are living in the past and not keeping up with the times. I know of churches going through these changes where pastors have told such people, "If you don't like it, you can leave!"

I heard one pastor, who was dramatically changing the direction of his church, preach a sermon in which he likened the situation to taking a flight on an airplane. "This is where this plane is going; so, if you don't like the destination, you ought to get off." Most of his lay leaders and most of the congregation got off! After shrinking his church down from a couple thousand to less than a couple hundred, He resigned and went elsewhere to pursue another ministry, leaving the devastation behind.[81]

---

[81] While on vacation, I was present in this service. Identity is reserved to protect the innocent involved.

Are we allowing Jesus Christ to build his church? Or are we 'doing church' in our own humanistic fashion? David Platt summarizes the way in which we view church today.

> I am part of the system that has created a whole host of means and methods, plans and strategies for doing church that require little if any power from God. And it's not just pastors who are involved in this charade. I am concerned that all of us - pastors and church members in our culture - have blindly embraced an American dream mentality that emphasizes our abilities and exalts our names in the ways we do church.
>
> Consider what it takes for successful businessmen and businesswomen, effective entrepreneurs and hard-working associates, shrewd retirees and idealistic students to combine forces with a creative pastor to grow a "successful church" today. Clearly it doesn't require the power of God to draw a crowd in our culture. A few key elements that we can manufacture will suffice.
>
> First, we need a good performance. In an entertainment driven culture, we need someone who can captivate the crowds. If we don't have a charismatic communicator, we are doomed. So even if we have to show him on a video screen, we must have a good preacher. It's even better if he has an accomplished worship leader with a strong band at his side.
>
> Next, we need a place to hold the crowds that will come, so we gather all our resources to

build a multi-million-dollar facility to house the performance . . .

Finally, once the crowds get there, we need to have something to keep them coming back. So we need to start programs – first-class, top-of-the-line programs . . . In order to have these programs, we need professionals to run them.[82]

David Platt further comments as he summarizes the scenario in many of our evangelical churches of today.

But what is strangely lacking in the picture of performances, personalities, programs, and professionals is desperation for the power of God. God's power is at best an add-on to our strategies. I am frightened by the reality that the church I lead can carry on most of our activities smoothly, efficiently, even successfully, never realizing that the Holy Spirit of God is virtually absent from the picture. We can so easily deceive ourselves, mistaking the presence of physical bodies in a crowd for the existence of spiritual life in a community.[83]

What Is Worship?

How do we define worship? This is where we must begin. If we do not define worship properly, we will soon fall into the trap of trivializing the worship of Almighty God.

---

[82] David Platt, IBID, pages 48-49
[83] David Platt, IBID, page 50

Too often, we use the term 'worship' to mean singing praises to God. This definition of worship is far too narrow and often leads to trivializing prayer and preaching.

A few years ago we were experiencing a severe drought in northern Arizona. The churches had called for a joint prayer meeting in a city park to pray for rain. There was a large gathering of Christians from the area and we began with small groups diligently seeking the Lord's presence and power. We spent at least 45 minutes worshiping the Lord in prayer and requesting that the Lord would have mercy upon our community and send us rain. A man came to the microphone with a guitar, and said to the crowd, "I think it's about time for us to worship!" It was obvious that his thinking about worship excluded the forty five minutes of prayer that the people had just experienced.

Jared C. Wilson comments on the problem of the church's narrow definition of worship.

> The dilution of the understanding of worship is a direct result of the dilution of theology in the church. The applicational, topical approach to Bible understanding has the consequence of making us think (and live) in segmented ways. The music leader takes the stage to say, "We're gonna start with a time of worship." Is the whole service not a time of worship? Isn't the sermon an act of worship?
>
> Isn't all of life meant to be an act of worship?
>
> One reason we have struggled to develop fully devoted followers of Jesus is that we incorrectly assign our terminology (equating worship with music only) and thereby train

our people to think in truncated, reductionistic ways.[84]

Public worship is the privilege and duty of redeemed souls, united in faith, fellowship and the furtherance of the gospel. But what is worship? How do you define worship of Jehovah?

Jesus responded to the woman at the well of Samaria, who questioned him about the place of worship. She drew attention to the fact that the Samaritans worshiped in Samaria, while the Jews worshiped in Jerusalem. Jesus quickly quelled her attention on the place of worship when he said, "The hour is coming, and now is, when the true worshipers will worship the Father in spirit and in truth; for the Father is seeking such to worship Him. God is Spirit, and those who worship Him must worship in spirit and truth."[85]

Worship is man's proper response to God's revelation of Himself. Man's proper response to God's revelation of Himself involves man's spirit. His heart must be right before God, leading him to repent from sin and yield himself completely to the Lord Jesus Christ. Worship involves man's emotions and his will. It is his effort to love the Lord God with all of his heart, mind and strength. The Holy Spirit enables the believer's spirit to worship properly and meaningfully.

A proper response of man to God's revelation of Himself involves the truth of God. One cannot truly worship God without understanding the truth about

---

[84] From website www.crossway.org: Taken from The Prodigal Church: A Gentle Manifesto against the Status Quo, by Jared C. Wilson. Used by permission of Crossway, a publishing ministry of Good News Publishers, Wheaton, Il 60187
[85] John, 4:23-24

God that is revealed in His holy word. Therefore, any definition of worship that excludes the preaching and teaching of God's word is faulty and inadequate.

Prayer Is Worship

When we pray, we are also worshiping. Our prayers must be molded and guided by the truth of God's word. In many modern evangelical churches, prayer seems to be inconsequential and almost non-existent.

How often in your church is there an invocation prayer? As we gather in the name of the Lord Jesus Christ, should we not come into His presence, invoking Him to manifest Himself to us? Is it not appropriate to claim His promise that where two or three are gathered in His name, there He will be in our midst? It has been a long time since I have heard a pastor or a worship leader lead us in an invocation prayer. An invocation prayer helps me to put aside all the distractions and to focus my attention upon Jesus Christ.

Benediction prayers are also missing from our Sunday gatherings. Whether it be directly from the Scripture, or a benediction prepared by the pastor or worship leader, a benediction sends believers out to face another week. When well prepared, a benediction prayer closes the worship service with dignity, reminding us that we are not alone, but that our God will be constantly watching over us and guiding us.

The pastoral prayer is almost a relic of the past. As believers gather together to worship the Lord, there are many who gather with heavy burdens and monumental concerns. It is impossible in larger congregations to pray for each individual need. However, when the pastor prays for categories of needs, it is very comforting to know that your needs are being lifted up to the Lord. A pastor can pause in his prayer, allowing a time of silence, encouraging each one to bring his personal burden and need to the Lord. The apostle Paul told the Philippian church, "Be anxious for nothing, but in everything by prayer and supplication, with thanksgiving, let your requests be made known to God; and the peace of God, which surpasses all understanding, will guard your hearts and minds through Christ Jesus."[86]

I have been in more worship services than I can count when the total time of praying has not exceeded more than two or three minutes. This is a travesty! Is it any wonder that our worship services are anemic and powerless? When the disciples walked with Jesus, they did not ask Him to teach them to preach. However, they did ask Him, "Teach us to pray!"

Preaching Is Worship

Preaching and teaching God's word must be an integral part of worship as God's people gather together. Jesus responded to Satan's temptation that "man shall not live by bread alone, but by every word that proceeds from the mouth of God." [87] There are starving sheep in the Lord's flocks today who long for biblical, expository preaching that feeds their souls?

David Platt challenges our comfortable Christianity in our Western world. He says:

---

[86] Philippians 4:6-7
[87] Matthew 4:4

This is the question that often haunts me when I stand before a crowd of thousands of people in the church I pastor. What if we take away the cool music and the cushioned chairs? What if the screens are gone and the stage is no longer decorated? What if the air-conditioning is off and the comforts are removed? Would His Word still be enough for His people to come together?[88]

Excluding the preaching and teaching of God's word from our definition of worship has led to the devaluation of preaching and the decline of biblical knowledge in the lives of believers. If worship is indeed man's proper response to God's revelation of Himself, how can we exclude preaching and teaching the word of God from our definition of worship? It is preaching and teaching of God's word that is the primary source of God's revelation of Himself.

The Worship Leader

Leading God's people in worship is an awesome responsibility. Almighty God, Father, Son and Holy Spirit is our audience. We are bringing our offerings of praise and responding to His truth. It is to be done decently and in order. It is also to be done with a right spirit as we approach our great God with humility and reverence.

Each one who has a part up front leading people in worship must come prepared in heart and mind. We must humbly submit ourselves to the Lord, seeking His power and His leading as we prepare our part for leading the corporate worship. Anyone who is

---

[88] David Platt, IBID, page 27

involved up front as a worship leader must be diligent in seeking the Lord's leading and guidance as you prepare the service. Do you come with a clean heart before the Lord? Are you truly worshiping the Lord yourself, or are you performing? Preacher, are you living what you are preaching? Have you let the Lord do His work in your own heart and life? Are you genuine in your living out the truth that you are sharing with the sheep?

In many churches entertainment and professionalism has replaced genuine worship. Often we have so 'modernized' our worship services that the power of the Holy Spirit is replaced by our methods. Substituting entertainment for experiencing 'the fear of the Lord' leaves us hollow and empty. We must not cheat people with the slick presentation in place of the awesome Presence of the Lord. We have come to depend upon our methods rather than the divine working of God's Holy Spirit.

Jim Cymbala, pastor of the Brooklyn Tabernacle in Brooklyn, New York, writes:[89]

> Over the last twenty five years, we have seen more church growth tools, books, conferences, and fads than in the entire history of our country. And yet we do not only have the loss in church attendance, we also have a decline in the spiritual fervor and study of the Bible by churchgoers.

The Music Issue

---

[89] Jim Cymbala, article in Decision magazine, December, 2014, page 9-11

Traditional churches and contemporary churches battle over music in worship. Older Christians, and many younger Christians, prefer the old hymns with which they are familiar. Many believers are drawn back to their faith formation, to their up-bringing, by familiar hymns that allow them to truly worship the Lord.

Most evangelical churches have moved away from using the hymns of the past in favor of contemporary choruses and worship songs. It is rare to be able to sing an old familiar hymn in churches today. Some of the words of old hymns appear in new packages and unfamiliar tunes.

Some churches seek to provide variety in their worship services. If they are large enough, they may provide a traditional service format and also a contemporary service format. Smaller churches, with only one worship service on Sunday mornings may seek to do a blended style of worship service.

It is not the style of music that determines whether one worships the Lord or not. Much has to do with the attitude with which the worshiper comes. The music that the worship leader selects is also important. Let's face it! There are some old hymns that are not usable in worship and there are many contemporary worship songs that ought to be cast on to the scrapheap. Many lyrics for hymns and worship choruses are not biblical in their content. Others that have biblical content have poor tunes that are not singable and are not conducive to corporate worship. Look around the congregation as you lead in worship. We must remember that, if the worshipers are not participating, we are failing in our efforts to lead God's people in honoring our God.

Different cultures have different styles of musical taste. When I am present with believers in some other country, even when I do not understand their language, I find that their worship style leads them to worship God in much different forms because of their cultural differences. In a similar way, our churches in the Western world are confronted with different sub-cultures, depending upon the age of congregants, as well as their different likes and dislikes. Psalm 150 exhorts us to praise and worship with all kinds of instruments, some of which were more acceptable to the Jewish culture of the Psalmist's day than to our present day culture.

Jim Cymbala continues in his writing:

> It is possible that one might think sound doctrinal preaching is enough, but Scripture shows us that we also need to rely on the Holy Spirit's power and direction.

> On another extreme, some contemporary churches have turned their focus to numerical growth at the expense of sound biblical practices. Whatever keeps people coming back for more next week seems primary, with barely a thought to what the "more" entails. More thought is given to the music, lights and production features than Bible teaching and prayer. Everything is filtered through the lens of whatever will make folks comfortable and not offended . . .

> Some of the traditionalist churches fault modern churches for diluting, or even ignoring, the word of God. They wonder how anyone can call a church "Christian" if Christ, salvation from sin and the meaning of the cross are ignored, and if preachers are more

like life coaches, than New Testament ministers. In some places, the effort to be seeker-sensitive and user-friendly has produced little, if any, resemblance to the Christian churches found in God's word.[90]

The Issue of Rock and Roll

Rock music and its use in Christian churches is one of the most controversial topics; however, it is a topic that we must not avoid. If you are one of the Christian worship leaders who favors the use of rock music with Christian words, I challenge you to openly consider whether rock music is an appropriate form for Christian worship.

For several decades now this has been debated by many. Those who advocate the use of rock music in Christian worship are convinced that music is neutral. They say it is the lyrics that determine whether it is proper for Christian worship. However, there are many secular musicians who believe that rock music has a beat that is designed to arouse people sexually. When you witness the dance that usually accompanies rock music, it is clearly sexually suggestive. The very term "rock 'n roll" described the sexual nature of this style of music.

John Blanchard, writing in 1983, says this about music in evangelism:

> If our analysis of rock music is right, using it in evangelism is spiritually perilous. But is it scripturally possible? Is there such a thing as 'Christian rock (or pop) music'? The way to begin answering that question is to ask a

---

[90] Jim Cymbala, IBID

much more fundamental one, which is this: Is there such a thing as 'Christian music' at all? What do we mean by the phrase? Are we describing the music? Take a sheet of music from a 'Christian song' and one from a 'secular song'. Are they essentially different? Is a B flat in a hymn any different from one in a bawdy rock number? Can you tell a Christian quaver from a non-Christian one? Is it something to do with the instruments? Is there such a thing as a godly guitar, a sanctified saxophone or a born again bassoon? Nobody is questioning the point that one can have Christian musicians, but the simple fact of the matter is that there is no such thing as 'Christian music'. There are Christians, and there is music; there is good music and there is bad music (and that statement has nothing to do with taste, style, culture, or the age of the performer or listener); there is music that reflects God's glory and music that does not. . . . Music is not 'good' because it is being performed in a religious context, any more than music is 'bad' because it is being performed in a 'secular' context. All these divisions tend to blur the truth. Music must be judged not by its context, but by its content. Beautiful flowers can be found in a dusty desert and poisonous plants in a lovely garden.[91]

While Blanchard does not completely rule out the use of rock music in evangelism, he cautions against it because of its hypnotic power which makes the listener unusually susceptible to whatever suggestions are made by the lyrics.

---

[91] Pop Goes the Gospel, John Blanchard, with Peter Anderson & Derek Cleave (evangelical press Durham, England, 1983), pages 27-28

While Dr. Martyn Lloyd-Jones is not writing, particularly about rock music, he does have something to say to preachers about manipulating people emotionally. He says:

> We can become drunk on music - there is no question about that. Music can have the effect of creating an emotional state in which the mind is no longer functioning as it should be, and no longer discriminating. I have known people to sing themselves into a state of intoxication without realizing what they were doing.

Dr. Martyn Lloyd-Jones is cautioning against spiritual decisions made in response to emotional, perhaps even hypnotic moods, rather than by rational thought. He further says, "The important point is that we should realize that the effect produced in such a case is not produced by the truth." [92]

Shelly Garlock Hamilton has written a brief book entitled, "Why I Don't Listen to Contemporary Christian Music."[93] Hamilton is a professionally trained musician who analyzes rock music and concludes that it is an inappropriate music style for Christian worship. She has interviewed many secular rock musicians, all of whom state unequivocally that rock music is sexual music.

Neil Postman, a former professor of communication at NYU, wrote in his book, Amusing Ourselves to Death, 1985, "to maintain that technology (which

---

[92] Dr. Martyn Lloyd-Jones, Preaching and Preachers, quoted by John Blanchard.

[93] Why I Don't Listen to Contemporary Christian Music, Shelly Garlock (Hamilton, Majesty Music, www.majestymusic.com, 733. Wade Hampton Blvd., Greenville, SC 29609)

includes music and entertainment) is neutral . . . is . . . stupidity, plain and simple."[94]

Luke Campbell of 2 Live Crew, record label owner and active as rap performer from 1985 until 2006, says about rock music, "the sex is definitely in the music, and sex in all aspects is in the rock music."[95]

John Oates, of Paul and Oates, American rock musician, songwriter and producer, from 1967 until the present, says, "Rock 'n' roll is 99% sex."[96]

Alan Bloom, professor of sociology at the University of Chicago, wrote in his book, The Closing of the American Mind, 1987,

> This is the significance of rock music. I do not suggest that it has any high intellectual sources. But it has risen to its current heights in the education of the young on the ashes of classical music, and in an atmosphere in which there is no intellectual resistance to attempts to tap the rawest passions . . . But rock music has one appeal only, a barbaric appeal to sexual desire - not love . . . but sexual desire, undeveloped and untutored. . . . Young people know that rock has the beat of sexual intercourse.[97]

Hamilton concludes her chapter on the rock beat with this assessment.

> I researched the topic, "sex and the rock beat," on the Internet. Seventy pages on the subject came up. There does not appear to be a dearth of material, if you are interested in

[94] IBID, page 22.
[95] IBID, page 29.
[96] IBID, page 29.
[97] IBID, pages 30, 31.

researching the topic for yourself. In these seventy pages, it is definite that the world believes rock music to be sensual. I've found that if the world, says something is sensual, given that they are sensually minded, they are "dead-on" correct. The world says, "tight and revealing" invokes sensual dress. Are they correct? In the statements quoted about the rock beat, the world says, "the rock beat" not only invokes sensual responses, but also is sex. I would say that they are again "dead-on" correct; and if they are correct, we can safely deduce that the rock beat, being sensual, does not line up with the biblical principles of holiness and purity.[98]

Dr. Henry M. Morris III makes this comment about worshiping as we sing the songs of Zion.

Herein lies the challenge for us. The 'sounds' of the world are everywhere. The 'noise' of evil is a strident screech that threatens to engulf any effort to sing the song of truth. But sing we must!

He then quotes Psalm 96:1-3.

Oh, sing to the Lord a new song! Sing to the Lord, all the earth. Sing to the Lord, bless his name; proclaim the good news of his salvation from day to day. Declare his glory among the nations, his wonders among all peoples.[99]

---

[98] IBID, pages 35-36.
[99] Dr. Henry M. Morris III, Article: Sounds of Music, Words of Truth (Acts & Facts magazine, published by Institute for Creation Research, Dallas, Texas August 2015, page 7

'Dressing Up' or 'Dressing Down'

How aught people to dress for church? The contemporary churches have gone the direction of 'dressing down' as we gather together, while the traditional churches have maintained 'dressing up' to honor the Lord by our best appearance. It is more common to see a pastor dressed casually as he preaches, than to see a pastor in a suit and tie. The argument seems to be that the pastor wants to make people feel comfortable no matter how they are dressed. We do not want to keep people from coming to church services because we insist that they be dressed a certain way.

Have we gone too far in this direction? As human beings, we tend to go to extremes. Are shorts and flip-flops the best we can do for our Lord? Are women learning to dress modestly, as pleasing to the Lord? The apostle Paul, writing to pastor Timothy, says: "in like manner also, that the women adorn themselves in modest apparel, with propriety and moderation, not with braided hair or gold or pearls or a costly clothing, but, which is proper for women professing godliness, with good works."[100]

In our culture today, male news anchors and sportscasters usually are dressed in suits and ties, while women news anchors and sportscasters usually are dressed neatly in dresses or pantsuits. While I am not suggesting that pastors who dress casually are dishonoring the Lord, I am questioning the extreme casualness of those who are representing Christ in the pulpit. When a pastor dresses in a T-shirt and blue-jeans with holes, it appears to me that he is treating his God assigned task of preaching the holy word of God as casual

---

[100] 1 Timothy 2:9-10

and unimportant. Does the way we dress say anything about how we represent Almighty God?

My father and mother, obviously from another era, taught their children to respect the Lord Jesus Christ and God our Father by dressing our best. We did not have much of this world's goods, however, they taught us that we should do our best to dress properly for church. They taught us that we were going to worship the King of Kings and the Lord of Lords! They insisted that we should dress appropriately.

Think about it! If you were invited into the presence of the Queen of England, or to the White House to visit the president of the United States, how would you dress? Would you dress in shorts and flip-flops? If you did, you probably would be turned away. I suspect you would put on your best clothes and seek to be very presentable in the presence of dignitaries. If you were appointed as an ambassador to another nation, representing the president of the United States, how would you dress when doing your work? Does not our Lord Jesus Christ deserve even more respect than earthly rulers and government authorities?

The apostle James clearly tells us that we are to treat all who come into our assemblies with respect and impartiality.[101] We are not to treat those who are rich in a better way than those who are poor. We must never turn away anyone from our assemblies because of the way they are dressed. However, this does not mean that all of us should dress sloppily just to make others feel comfortable. When a worship leader stands up front to lead us in honoring the Lord, his manner of dress ought to

---

[101] James 2:1-8

show respect for the Lord. A pastor, speaking forth the word of God, must be dressed in such a way as to represent his Lord appropriately.

Even the Federal prisons demand conformance to a dress code. This is the dress Code instructions from the Federal Prison internet site.

U. S. Department of Justice
Federal Bureau of Prisons
Federal Correctional Institution
Oxford, Wisconsin 53952

Inmates will inform prospective visitors that dress should be within the bounds of good taste, and should not present disrespect to others who may be present in the visiting room. Any clothing which is suggestive, provocative or revealing is not suitable for the visiting room environment. All visitors, regardless of age, will have to abide by these rules. Visitors who prefer to wear dresses or skirts may do so provided the hem line is knee length when seated. Capris may be worn provided they are below the knee when seated. All visitors must wear shoes. Visitors may be denied a visit at the front lobby if it is determined a visitor's clothing is inappropriate for the institution setting.

The following items ARE NOT permitted in the visiting room:
Sleeveless shirts,
Halter, tank or tube tops,
Shirts/blouses with plunging necklines,
Transparent/see-through clothing,
Spandex/form fitting clothing,
Clothing with holes,
Hats, caps or shirts with hoods,

Khaki colored clothing,
Camouflage clothing,
Shorts of any color (for adults and children 3 years or older),
Coats, jackets, gloves or scarves (any type of outdoor apparel),
Flip flops or shower shoes,
Food is not allowed to be brought into the visiting room,
No photos, papers, newspaper clippings, etc.
No open-toed or open-heel shoes.

Do you dress up or dress down when you go to church? This is not a matter of right or wrong, good or evil. How you answer this question depends, to some degree, upon the culture that you live in. However, your answer must be guided by some principles of Scripture that are laid down by the apostle Paul regarding "disputable or doubtful matters".[102] We are not to be judgmental of each other, allowing for freedom in Christ. This freedom of choice, however, is to be curtailed by our consideration of others. We are not to be stumbling blocks to other believers. This requires that we dress modestly in order to not interfere with the worship of our brothers and sisters. Modest dressing is to be practiced by all believers whether in church or elsewhere in public.

Worship is primarily a matter of the heart. The heart must be right before God and our hearts must be right in our consideration of fellow believers. We must not discount the importance of dressing respectfully and appropriately as believers by saying, "Well, my heart is right!" Jennifer Maggio gives this perspective:

---

[102] Romans 14

I love makeup. I love high heels and beautiful blouses. I love a new haircut, a sparkly-pocketed pair of blue jeans, and great new boots. And I do not think there is anything wrong with any of those things. But when the shirt covering our hearts becomes more important than the purity therein, it is a major problem. When the heart that graces our inside is less important than the new necklace draped across its outside, we are in dangerous territory.[103]

I do not think it is expecting too much, as followers of Jesus Christ, to dress appropriately when we come to the Lord's house to worship the Lord our God. Again Jennifer Maggio concludes this matter well.

If your desire is to put on a pant suit or full-length church dress because you believe that brings honor to your Savior, then, please do so. But be careful not to pass judgment on the young mom across the aisle who wears jeans and a tattered t-shirt. Spend more time preparing your heart for the message that the pastor will be bringing, rather than ironing your attire. Spend more time praying for the worship leader, rather than choosing just the right jewelry for your Sunday outfit. And above all else, bring with you a pure heart, ready to gather in the King's house and welcome all in, regardless of how they are dressed.[104]

---

[103] Jennifer Maggio, What You are Wearing to Church, (an article posted by Crosswords.com, June 15, 2015, previously posted on iBelieve.com)
[104] Jennifer Maggio, IBID

Worship of our God is the greatest and most important thing that we do with our lives! Let's be certain that we are not trivializing corporate worship.

Chapter 5

The Pulpit and Preaching

Preaching has fallen on hard times in the churches of the Western world. Most of what is called preaching in our American evangelical churches is a 'pabulum' diet that does very little to develop a mature faith in the believers. The sheep of God's pasture are given a regular diet of shallow homilies, laced with interesting or humorous stories, rather than good expositional preaching. Thankfully there are still a few preachers who are faithfully preaching God's word and seeking to do solid exposition of Scripture.

Dr. James McDonald, senior pastor of Harvest Bible Church, Rolling Meadows, Illinois writes this about preaching.

> Drafting off Chesterton's word choice, is biblical preaching rejected because it is tried and found lacking or because it is found difficult and therefore not tried? Biblical preaching demands effort, drains energy, and distracts attention away from other things that matter too, but demand less. Real preaching requires any offense to be resolved, sin to be surrendered, and distraction to be diminished. It's easy to do poorly and terrifically difficult to do well, once. The better you preach, the greater the demand that you do it great, again next week, because "we are bringing our friends." No matter how good the meal, take a deep breath, because they will be just as hungry in less than seven days, and you need to know you "have it" well before then. Good preaching is a love-hate relationship: I love

preaching, I hate preparing; I love seeing God work, I hate the pressure of needing to see it again; I love the Lord and his word, I hate the battle he allows to accompany its proclamation. [105]

Many church ministries today are little more than 'pop- psychology' or 'positive-thinking' factories that seek to motivate people to do their best, trust the Lord and He will bless you abundantly. For after all, God is on your side and values you so much that He will not withhold health and prosperity from all who seek Him. These ministries appeal to the old human nature. Such preachers are preaching what people want to hear. Such preaching tickles the ear but famishes the soul.

Joel Osteen's ministry caught the focus of attention, as his wife, Victoria shared her message with their massive congregation. She wanted them to realize that their devotion to God is not really about God, but about themselves.

> I just want to encourage every one of us to realize when we obey God, we're not doing it for God - I mean, that's one way to look at it - we're doing it for ourselves, because God takes pleasure when we are happy . . . That's the thing that gives Him the greatest joy.
>
> So, I want you to know this morning - Just do good for your own self. Do good because God wants you to be happy . . . When you come to church, when you worship Him, you're not doing it for God really. You're doing it for yourself, because that's what makes God happy. Amen?

---

[105] James McDonald, Vertical Church, (David C Cook, copyright 2012), page 199

102

Joel Osteen's ministry is only one of many such ministries in our Western world. Dr. Albert Mohler comments in one of his blogs as he analyzes such ministries.

America deserves the Osteens. The consumer culture, the cult of the therapeutic, the marketing impulse and the sheer superficiality of American cultural Christianity probably made the Osteens inevitable. The Osteens are phenomenally successful because they are the exaggerated fulfillment of the self-help movement and the cult of celebrity rolled into one massive megachurch media empire. And, to cap it all off, they give Americans what Americans crave - reassurance delivered with a smile.

Judged in theological terms, the Osteen message is the latest and slickest version of Prosperity Theology. That American heresy has now spread throughout much of the world, but it began in the context of American Pentecostalism in the early 20th century. Prosperity theology, promising that God rewards faith with health and wealth, first appealed to those described as "the dispossessed" - the very poor.

Now, its updated version appeals to the aspirational class of the suburbs. Whereas the early devotees of prosperity theology prayed for a roof over their heads that did not leak, the devotees of prosperity theology in the Age of Osteen pray for ever bigger houses. The story of how the Osteens exercised faith for a big house comes early in Joel Osteen's best-seller, Your Best Life Now.[106]

Does your preaching result in your people maturing in Christ, so that whatever comes in life, they will be able to stand true to the Lord? How would your preaching be accepted in countries where believers are suffering for their faith, some even paying with their own lives for their faithful allegiance to their Lord and Savior, Jesus Christ? How does prosperity preaching sound to their suffering ears? True preaching of the word of God must not exclude suffering and persecution. After all, the Lord Jesus Christ himself said, "In this world you will have tribulation; but be of good cheer, I have overcome the world."[107]

David Platt challenges us to think about the gospel that we are preaching in our Western world churches. We would do well to consider his challenge in order to be certain that we are establishing God's people as true disciples (obedient followers) of Jesus Christ, rather than simply encouraging cultural Christians.

> We are giving into the dangerous temptation to take the Jesus of the Bible and twist him into a version of Jesus, we are more comfortable with.

> A nice, middle-class, American Jesus. A Jesus who doesn't mind materialism and who would never call us to give away everything we have. A Jesus who would not expect us to forsake our closest relationships so that He receives all our affection. A Jesus who is fine

---

[106] The Osteen Predicament: Mere Happiness Cannot Bear the Weight of the Gospel, blog by Albert Mohler, 9/10/2014
[107] John 16:33

with nominal devotion that does not infringe on our comforts, because, after all, he loves us just the way we are. A Jesus who wants us to be balanced, who wants us to avoid dangerous extremes, and who, for that matter, wants us to avoid danger altogether. A Jesus who brings us comfort and prosperity, as we live out our Christian spin on the American dream.

But do you and I realize what we are doing at this point? We are molding Jesus into our image. He is beginning to look a lot like us because, after all, that is whom we are most comfortable with. And the danger now is that when we gather in our church buildings to sing and lift up our hands and worship, we may not actually be worshiping the Jesus of the Bible. Instead, we may be worshiping ourselves. [108]

Why is Preaching in Decline?

The removal of the pulpit from most contemporary churches is a symbol of the decline of preaching. During the period called the dark ages, the pulpit had been moved to the side while the mass became the center of the services. The reformers brought the pulpit back front and center of the church building. The preaching of the word of God was once more restored to its rightful place.

The apostle Paul states the priority of preaching the gospel of Jesus Christ.

---

[108] David Platt, Radical, (Multnomah Press, Colorado Springs, CO 80921), 2010, page 13.

For Christ did not send me to baptize, but to preach the gospel, not with wisdom of words, lest the cross of Christ should be made of no effect. For the message of the cross is foolishness to those who are perishing, but to us who are being saved it is the power of God . . . For since, in the wisdom of God, the world through wisdom did not know God, it pleased God through the foolishness of the message preached to save those who believe.[109]

There are several reasons leading to the trivializing of preaching in our churches today.

First, we have lost confidence in preaching the word of God because we are told that preaching is passé. We are told that people learn in a variety of ways, and one of the poorest ways of learning is lecture. Therefore many pastors have moved away from expositional preaching of the word of God in favor of interesting but shallow homilies, with a few attached Scripture verses to give the appearance of preaching the word. Pastors, let me ask you, "Could it be that you have lost confidence in the power of the word of God?" Have you lost your faith in the promise of our God, given by Isaiah, "So shall my word be that goes forth from my mouth; it shall not return to me void, but it shall accomplish what I please, and it shall prosper in the thing for which I sent it."[110]

The writer of Hebrews reminds us of the power of the word of God. He says, "For the word of God is living and powerful, and sharper than any two-edged sword, piercing even to the division of soul and spirit, and of joints and marrow, and is a

---

[109] 1 Corinthians 1:17-18, 21
[110] Isaiah 55:11

discerner of the thoughts and intents of the heart."[111]

Here is a second reason for the decline of biblical preaching. We as pastors have allowed ourselves to be moved away from one of our primary tasks. We have allowed ourselves to become CEO's rather than pastors. Our time and our passion is taken up by so many other tasks, such as managing the affairs of the church, that we neglect to carve out sufficient time to adequately prepare solid expositional messages. Good biblical preaching requires much prayer-bathed study to adequately interpret the text of Scripture and to present a well-organized sermon that is faithful to the portion of Scripture being preached.

The third reason is the failure of our seminaries and Bible colleges to prepare their graduates with the tools for the task of preaching. Have we come to see the task of pastoring a church and preaching God's word as a profession or a career, rather than a calling? If you are a pastor and you are viewing your role as a means of making a living, or as a professional career, you should leave the pastoral ministry and pursue some other line of work.

The Call to Preach

God calls certain people to preach the word and God equips those whom He calls. The call to preach the word is an inescapable compulsion. The one called by God to preach will know the same compulsion that the apostle Paul expresses in 1 Corinthians 6:16, "For if I preach the gospel, I have nothing to boast of, for necessity is laid upon me; yes, woe is me if I do not preach the gospel!"

---

[111] Hebrews 4:12

Our Bible colleges and seminaries have the responsibility to verify that their students are genuinely called of God to the sacred work of preaching God's word. They also must accept responsibility for teaching them how to interpret the word of God correctly and how to preach the word of God. They must be taught how to "be diligent to present yourself approved to God, a worker who does not need to be ashamed, rightly dividing the word of truth."[112]

Dr. Albert Mohler, president of Southern Baptist Seminary, writes this about a call to ministry.

> First, there is an inward call. Through His Spirit, God speaks to those persons He has called to serve as pastors and ministers of His Church. The great Reformer Martin Luther described this inward call as "God's voice heard by faith." Those whom God has called know this call by a sense of leading, purpose, and growing commitment.
>
> Charles Spurgeon identified the first sign of God's call to the ministry as "an intense, all-absorbing desire for the work." Those called by God sense a growing compulsion to preach and teach the Word, and to minister to the people of God.
>
> This sense of compulsion should prompt the believer to consider whether God may be calling him to the ministry. Has God gifted you with the fervent desire to preach? Has He equipped you with the gifts necessary for ministry? Do you love God's Word and feel

---

[112] 2 Timothy 2:15

called to teach? Spurgeon warned those who sought his counsel not to preach if they could help it. "But," Spurgeon continued, "if he cannot help it, and he must preach or die, then he is the man." That sense of urgent commission is one of the central marks of an authentic call.

Second, there is the external call. Baptists believe that God uses the congregation to "call out the called" to ministry. The congregation must evaluate and affirm the calling and gifts of the believer who feels called to the ministry. As a family of faith, the congregation should recognize and celebrate the gifts of ministry given to its members, and take responsibility to encourage those whom God has called to respond to that call with joy and submission.

These days, many persons think of careers rather than callings. The biblical challenge to "consider your call" should be extended from the call to salvation to the call to the ministry. [113]

John Newton, famous for writing "Amazing Grace," once remarked: "None but He who made the world can make a Minister of the Gospel." Unless you are truly called by God and equipped by God to preach the gospel, you'll be totally frustrated; and you will also be a frustration to the congregation which you are seeking to feed.

What is Preaching?

---

[113] http://www.albertmohler.com/2013/07/19/has-god-called-you-discerning-the-call-to-preach-2/

What is preaching? Is it simply a lecture? Is it simply giving a talk on a biblical subject? No! This is where we often go astray in this great task of preaching the word of God.

Preaching has a divine element to it or it is not preaching. Unless the preacher is led, inspired by and empowered by the Holy Spirit of God, the preacher may give a lecture, but he is not preaching. True biblical preaching is the truth of God, gleaned from the word of God, proclaimed through the man of God! Do you seek the anointing of the Holy Spirit every time you preach? The preacher, who is anointed by the Holy Spirit, will never be boring, nor dispassionate. He will be 'on fire' with the urgency of communicating God's word to his flock.

Jesus, when attending the synagogue in Nazareth, took the scroll and read the following from Isaiah 61, "The Spirit of the Lord is upon me, because He has anointed me to preach the gospel to the poor; He has sent me to heal the brokenhearted, to proclaim liberty to the captives, and recovery of sight to the blind, to set at liberty those who are oppressed, to proclaim the acceptable year of the Lord."[114] The Spirit of God is pleased to anoint you as you preach the gospel of Jesus Christ. It is this anointing of the Holy Spirit that is the difference between biblical preaching and an interesting talk or lecture.

The task of pastoring the flock of God's sheep and preaching the word of God is so overwhelming to the one who is called to this task. Each time that a pastor gets up to preach the word of God, he must come to the end of any self-dependence. He must genuinely, and humbly acknowledge that he, in and

---

[114] Luke 4:16-21

of himself, is not capable of fulfilling the calling of the Lord. He must fling himself totally upon the Lord Jesus Christ and the Holy Spirit of God. He must see himself as totally useless unless the Holy Spirit shows up. He must fully believe that the Holy Spirit will use him as an instrument to proclaim the truth of God from His word. He must then by faith proclaim the word of God, trusting that the Holy Spirit will do His work in the hearts of his audience.

There are some who believe that depending upon the Holy Spirit's anointing means that one does not need to prepare to preach. Some even go to the extreme that it is wrong to prepare because that shows you are not depending upon the Holy Spirit. Some use the words of Jesus to his disciples when he told them, "Now when they bring you to the synagogues and magistrates and authorities, do not worry about how or what you should answer, or what you should say. For the Holy Spirit will teach you in that very hour what you ought to say."[115] This is a promise to us when we have no time to prepare. It is a wonderful promise when we are surprised by an opportunity, perhaps even caused by persecution and oppression. We can be assured that the Lord will undertake through the Holy Spirit's power and presence. He will fill our mouths with the appropriate words.

However, this is no promise to the lazy and undisciplined pastor. Our responsibility is to study and pray in preparation for preaching and teaching the word of God. Rightly interpreting the word of God comes from much diligent study on the part of the preacher.[116]

---

[115] Luke 12:11-12
[116] 2 Timothy 2:14-15

The preacher must give all the glory to the Lord Jesus for all that He does through him. While it is exhilarating to be used as an instrument by God, the preacher must never take the credit to himself. He must remember that the Lord will never share His glory with another. James S. Stewart shares this perspective about preaching.

> There is no reason why your ministry should not achieve visible results, provided you keep alive within you a sense of the wonder of the facts you preach and of the urgency of the issues with which you deal. Every Sunday morning when it comes ought to find you awed and thrilled by the reflection -God is to be in action today, through me, for these people: this day may be crucial, this service decisive, for someone now ripe for the vision of Jesus.[117]

Power of Preaching Through Prayer

True prayer is a lifestyle, not simply an activity. To become a lifestyle, prayer requires discipline. It is not just the discipline of spending an amount of time in conscious prayer. It is the discipline of carving out a significant amount of time in each busy day to commune with God. The pastor who has not learned the work of prayer in his life is powerless in his preaching.

True prayer leads a pastor to bow his life before Almighty God and worship God as He is revealed in Scripture. The pastor must personally know God through experiencing His presence. Through communion with his Savior, the pastor must keep

---

[117] Stewart, James S. Heralds of God: A Practical Book on Preaching. (Reprint. Vancouver, BC: Regent Publishing, 2001) (1946), page 47

his life clean from all the garbage of the world. Through submission to Almighty God, Father, Son and Holy Spirit, he must know his weakness and acknowledge that without Him, he can do nothing. In his communion with God, the pastor must throw himself completely upon God to graciously mold his life, making him a useable instrument in the awesome task of preaching God's word.

A.W. Tozer, noted preacher of the past, says it well.

> To pray successfully is the first lesson the preacher must learn if he is to preach fruitfully; yet prayer is the hardest thing he will ever be called upon to do and, being human, it is the one act he will be tempted to do less frequently than any other. He must set his heart to conquer by prayer, and that will mean that he must first conquer his own flesh, for it is the flesh that hinders prayer always.

> Almost anything associated with the ministry may be learned with an average amount of intelligent application. It is not hard to preach or manage church affairs or pay a social call; weddings and funerals may be conducted smoothly with a little help from Emily Post and the Minister's Manual. Sermon making can be learned as easily as shoemaking - introduction, conclusion and all. And so with the whole work of the ministry as it is carried on in the average church today.

> But prayer - that is another matter. There Mrs. Post is helpless and the Minister's Manual can offer no assistance. There the lonely man of God must wrestle it out alone, sometimes in fastings and tears and weariness untold. There every man must be an original, for true prayer

cannot be imitated nor can it be learned from someone else. Everyone must pray as if he alone could pray, and his approach must be individual and independent; independent, that is, of everyone but the Holy Spirit.

Thomas à Kempis says that the man of God ought to be more at home in his prayer chamber than before the public. It is not too much to say that the preacher who loves to be before the public is hardly prepared spiritually to be before them. Right praying may easily make a man hesitant to appear before an audience. The man who is really at home in the presence of God will find himself caught in a kind of inward contradiction. He is likely to feel his responsibility so keenly that he would rather do almost anything than face an audience; and yet the pressure upon his spirit may be so great that wild horses could not drag him away from his pulpit.

No man should stand before an audience who has not first stood before God. Many hours of communion should precede one hour in the pulpit. The prayer chamber should be more familiar than the public platform. Prayer should be continuous, preaching but intermittent.[118]

Roy Laurin tells this story in his commentary on the book of Acts.

---

[118] Conquer by Prayer by A.W. Tozer. From the internet. A.W. Tozer (1897-1963) began his lifelong pursuit of God after hearing a street preacher in Akron, Ohio, at the age of seventeen. The self-taught theologian committed his life to the ministry of God's Word as a pastor, teacher, and writer.

Years ago, in New York City, a massive new organ was to be dedicated in a certain church. Everyone had come to hear a guest musician play the familiar songs of the sanctuary on the huge console. The service began, and as the organist pressed his fingers to the keys, he was horrified to find that not one single musical note would come forth. He pressed the start button, but still nothing happened. Then the custodian, sensing that the electricity had not been turned on, wrote a hasty note and handed it to the organist, telling him that after the invocation, the generator would be on and he could proceed with the service. The note read: After the prayer, the power will be on.

Biblical Preaching is Christo-Centric

Biblical expositional preaching must be Christo-centric; that is, it must always lead us to exalt Jesus Christ and to lift Him up as the only Savior and exalted Lord. There is no other way to the heavenly Father except through Jesus Christ, His son. The Old Testament points forward to the coming of the Messiah. The New Testament discloses that Messiah has come and that Jesus Christ is the Messiah. Therefore, whatever portion of the word of God that we are preaching, we must be certain that we are leading people to see Christ as Savior and Lord, and that we are leading God's redeemed people to be more faithful doers of the word.

Nehemiah was a leader of the Jews who had returned from captivity in Babylon. He led them to rebuild the walls of Jerusalem. After the walls were rebuilt, Nehemiah was burdened that the people would follow God's law. So he gathered the people together, men, women and children, to hear the law

115

read and explained. Ezra, and several of the Levites, read the word of God to the people. They also explained the meaning of God's word, so that the people would understand the sense of God's word. In Nehemiah 8:7-8, we read, they "helped the people to understand the law; and the people stood in their place. So they read distinctly from the book, in the law of God; and they gave the sense, and helped them to understand the reading."

I like what S. M. Lockridge says that a sermon ought to do. There are four things that a biblical sermon should accomplish.

> 1. A sermon should instruct the mind. You ought to learn something.
> 2. A sermon should tan your hide. It ought to correct you.
> 3. A sermon should warm your heart. It ought to inspire you.
> 4. A sermon should provoke your will. It ought to challenge you to do what the Lord wants you to do.[119]

Every pastor should seriously meditate on what the apostle Paul wrote to his son in-the-faith, Timothy. Take this as a challenge to you personally from our Lord Jesus Christ through the apostle Paul.

> I charge you, therefore, before God and the Lord Jesus Christ, who will judge the living and the dead at His appearing and His kingdom: Preach the word! Be ready in Season and out of season. Convince, rebuke, exhort, with all long-suffering and teaching. For the time will come when they will not endure sound doctrine, but according to their

---

[119] S.M. Lockridge, IBID

own desires, because they have itching ears, they will heap up for themselves teachers; and they will turn their ears away from the truth, and be turned aside to fables. That you be watchful in all things, endure afflictions, do the work of an evangelist, fulfill your ministry.[120]

To be a minister of the gospel called by Jesus Christ requires careful stewardship of God's gifts given to you by the Holy Spirit to equip you for the task. Your call from God is not for the timid, or for the lazy, or for those who are seeking worldly gain. Consider the words of the apostle Paul as he writes of his own stewardship of ministry.

I now rejoice in my sufferings for you, and fill up in my flesh, what is lacking in the afflictions of Christ, for the sake of His body, which is the church, of which I became a minister, according to the stewardship from God which was given to me for you, to fulfill the word of God, the mystery, which has been hidden from ages and from generations, but now has been revealed to his saints. To them, God willed to make known what are the riches of the glory of this mystery among the Gentiles: which is Christ in you, the hope of glory. Him we preach, warning every man, and teaching every man in all wisdom, that we may present every man perfect in Christ Jesus. To this end, I also labor, striving according to his working which works in me mightily.[121]

Some Practical Words for Preachers

[120] 2 Timothy 4:1-6
[121] Colossians 1:24-29

In today's churches pastors are reluctant to preach doctrine and theology. Many who teach preaching will tell pastors not to use theological language. Don't use words like 'saved' because they don't mean anything to the average listener. However, words like 'saved' or 'salvation' are good biblical words. It is the pastor's responsibility to explain these words and to teach what is meant by these scriptural terms.

The pastor must be a preacher of sound doctrine. This often requires the exposing and silencing of false teachers who seek to lead the flock astray. As Paul writes to Titus, a fellow bishop (overseer), he shares with him some of the qualities that are needed for such a task.

> For a bishop must be blameless, as a steward of God, not self-willed, not quick-tempered, not given to wine, not violent, not greedy for money, but hospitable, a lover of what is good, sober-minded, just, holy, self-controlled, holding fast the faithful word as he has been taught, that he may be able, by sound doctrine, both to exhort and convict those who contradict. For there are many insubordinate, both idle talkers and deceivers, especially those of the circumcision, whose mouths must be stopped, who subvert whole households, teaching things which they ought not, for the sake of dishonest gain. . . . This testimony is true. Therefore, rebuke them sharply, that they may be sound in the faith, not giving heed to Jewish fables and commandments of men who turned from the truth. [122]

---

[122] Titus 1:7-12, 14

A pastor's preaching of the word of God must come from an authentic obedient heart. You cannot effectively preach what you are not seeking to live out in your own walk with the Lord.

The 17th century pastor and preacher, John Owen says it well:

> A man preacheth that sermon only well unto others which preacheth itself in his own soul. And he that doth not feed on and thrive in the digestion of the food which he provides for others will scarce make it savoury unto them . . . If the word does not dwell with power in us, it will not pass with power from us.[123]

Good biblical preaching should be done authoritatively. Peter says that "If anyone speaks, let him speak as the oracles of God."[124] The apostle Paul wrote to Titus, "Speak these things, and exhort, and rebuke with all authority. Let no one despise you."[125]

Most of the Scripture is crystal clear in its meaning and in its message. Whenever the word of God is crystal clear, the pastor has the responsibility of preaching the word with the authority of God. There ought to be no doubt "thus saith the Lord!" This does not mean that the pastor should be dogmatic on every topic. There are some passages of Scripture that lend themselves to different interpretations. The preacher can be authoritative, without being dogmatic in all things.

---

[123] Quote from John Owen is from Chapter V, The True Nature of a Gospel Church, The Works of John Owen, volume 16 (Carlisle, PA: The Banner of Truth Trust, 1968).
[124] 1 Peter 4:11
[125] Titus 2:15

The process of God communicating with man through the man of God is called preaching. It is proclaiming or heralding forth the message of God. There is an urgency about preaching. There is a necessity that God's message be clearly proclaimed so that there can be no doubt about what He says. Each time that a pastor gets up to preach the word of God, he must do so with burning in his heart to have the people understand this great word of God. So work at your craft of preaching. If you do so, people will not be bored; they will return over and over again to hear a word from the Lord through His servant who is passionate for His Master.

The apostle Paul challenges the church at Rome,

> For whoever calls on the name of the Lord shall be saved. How then shall they call on him in whom they have not believed? And how shall they believe in him of whom they have not heard? And how shall they hear without a preacher? And how shall they preach unless they are sent? As it is written: 'how beautiful are the feet of those who preach the gospel of peace, who bring glad tidings of good things!' [126]

As Richard Baxter once said, "Preach as never sure to preach again, as a dying man to dying men."[127]

---

[126] Romans 10:13-15
[127] Quoted in I. D. E. Thomas, A Puritan Golden Treasury (Carlisle, PA: The Banner of Truth Trust, 1977) p. 223.

Chapter 6

CEO or Pastor

What does it mean to be a pastor? How does a pastor maintain his integrity and his character? What is the task to which a pastor is called? What are the duties that a pastor must fulfill?

In our Western world churches, many pastors are losing their way when it comes to fulfilling the biblical pattern of pastor. The biblical pastoral role has been trivialized or overshadowed by the modern day pastoral expectations of churches.

Many are the older born-again believers who have left our evangelical churches who are disillusioned with the church. They feel devalued by pastors who are focusing intensely upon changing their worship services to cater only to the younger generation. It is not that they are opposed to some change in music style, as long as their preference of the older hymns is not simply cast aside. When they are told directly by pastoral leadership and by church board leadership, "If you don't like it, go somewhere else!" what message does this convey? In some church growth seminars, church leaders are being told, "If you want to reach the younger generation, you must be willing to sacrifice many of the older people who are opposed to change." This is not the way to treat sincere older believers who have stood by their church for many years, supporting it with their prayers, their service and their money.

It is not only the style of music used in worship services that is the problem. Nor is it only the older people who are becoming disillusioned with the organized evangelical churches. There are also some younger people who struggle with the direction of the evangelical churches. A major problem is the attitude of church leaders toward the flock over which the Lord has given them oversight. It is the feeling of many Christians today that the church they have attended for many years is no longer concerned about them and their needs. They are feeling abandoned by those whom they feel should care the most. Many pastors and church leaders are focused more upon building spectacular, entertaining services than they are about loving and ministering to their people.

Jared Wilson writes about the alarming trend in our churches as we look for pastors to lead us.

> Our shepherds are increasingly hired for their dynamic speaking or catalytic leadership rather than their commitment to and exposition of the Scriptures, and for their laboring in the increase of attendance rather than the increase of gospel proclamation.
>
> Now, of course, none of those contrasted qualities are mutually exclusive. Pastors can be both skillful managers and biblically wise; they can be both great speakers and great students of Scripture; and they can both attract crowds and proclaim the gospel. The problem is that, while they are not mutually exclusive, the latter qualities in each contrast have lost priority and consequently have lost favor. We have not prospered theologically or spiritually when we emphasize the professionalization of the pastorate.[128]

---

[128] Taken from: The Prodigal Church: A Gentle Manifesto against the Status Quo, by Jared C. Wilson. Crossway, a

Pastor John S. Dickerson comments on the condition of the evangelical churches of America.

> The body is bleeding out because its leaders, its servants, and its people have forgotten how to make disciples as Jesus described and modeled.
>
> We can call it shepherding. We can call it discipleship. We can even call it being relational. What the three have in common is real people dealing with real life, together - and pointing each other to Jesus as they do. What we are failing at is real ministry. Not commercial or mass-marketed events, but real ministry and real lives - the way, Paul, Peter, John, and even Jesus did it. We have somehow lost it on a large scale.[129]

Our Lord and our Savior, Jesus Christ, the head of the church, has told us how we will be identified as His disciples. He said, "By this all will know that you are My disciples, if you have love for one another."[130] The word 'love', in this verse, is from the Greek word 'agapao' which is much more than emotional brotherly love. It is a love that is based upon valuing another person to the point that you will intentionally make an effort to understand that person, to care for that person and to seek to meet that person's need. When this kind of love is lacking within the church body, it is often because the pastors and other church leaders are not

publishing ministry of Good News Publishers, Wheaton, Il 60187, www.crossway.org.
[129] John S. Dickerson, The Great Evangelical Recession; (Baker Books, Grand Rapids, Michigan), 2013, page 183
[130] John 13:35

developing this kind of culture within the body. In this they must be an example to the flock.

Examine The Pastor's Role Biblically

There are three words used in the New Testament to refer to this office within the church of Jesus Christ. They are all used interchangeably, each having a different emphasis.

The first word is 'elder'. Elder is the translation of the Greek word 'presbuteros'. The apostle Paul wrote to Titus, telling him that he had left him in Crete, "that you should set in order the things that are lacking, and appoint elders in every city, as I commanded you."[131]

Many interpret this to mean that every church is to have multiple elders. This is not necessarily a proper interpretation. When we consider that the early churches gathered primarily in homes, and that there were probably several home-based congregations in every city, it is more likely that each home church was to have a pastor. He is called an elder. The elder that Titus was to appoint was to be the pastor of the church that met in someone's home. Paul does not use the term 'pastor' as he writes to Titus, however, he does use the word 'bishop' in the following verses. Obviously in the context, 'bishop' is the same person who is referred to as 'elder' in verse five. He was to be a mature believer whose qualifications are described by the apostle Paul as he writes to Titus.

> If a man is blameless, the husband of one wife, having faithful children not accused of dissipation or insubordination. For a bishop

---

[131] Titus 1:5

must be blameless, as a steward of God, not self-willed, not quick-tempered, not given to wine, not violent, not greedy for money, but hospitable, a lover of what is good, sober-minded, just, holy, self-controlled, holding fast the faithful word as he has been taught, that he may be able, by sound doctrine, both to exhort and convict those who contradict.[132]

The apostle Paul expands the qualifications for a bishop as he writes to Timothy.

This is a faithful saying: if a man desires the position of a bishop, he desires a good work. A bishop then must be blameless, the husband of one wife, temperate, sober minded, of good behavior, hospitable, able to teach; not given to wine, not violent, not greedy for money, but gentle, not quarrelsome, not covetous; one who rules his own house well, having his children in submission with all reverence (for if a man does not know how to rule his own house, how will he take care of the Church of God?); Not a novice, lest being puffed up with pride he fall into the same condemnation as the devil. Moreover he must have a good testimony among those who are outside, lest he fall into reproach and the snare of the devil.[133]

The second word used of the same office as elder is 'bishop' or 'overseer'. Bishop is the translation from the Greek word 'episcopos'. The 'overseer' is the official leader of the local congregation of believers. The apostle Peter makes it abundantly clear that the overseer or bishop is not a dictator who rules with an iron hand. He is not to "lord it

---

[132] Titus 1:6-9
[133] 1 Timothy 3:1-7

over those entrusted to you, but being examples to the flock . . ."[134]

The third word used is 'pastor' or 'shepherd'. This word is from the Greek word 'poimen' and it refers to the functional aspects or the work of the elder or bishop. W. E. Vine says, "Pastors guide as well as feed the flock; compare Acts 20:28, which, with verse 17, indicates that this was the service committed to elders (overseers or bishops); so also in 1 Peter 5:1, 2, "Tend the flock . . . exercising the oversight," this involves tender care and vigilant superintendence."[135]

This word 'poimen' is used by the apostle Paul in Ephesians 4 where he explains the functioning of the New Testament church. Paul links together 'pastor and teacher' as he speaks of this Spirit-gifted individual given by God to his church.

> And He Himself gave some to be apostles, some prophets, some evangelists, and some pastors and teachers, for the equipping of the saints for the work of ministry, for the edifying of the body of Christ, till we all come to the unity of the faith and of the knowledge of the Son of God, to a perfect man, to the measure of the stature of the fullness of Christ; that we should no longer be children, tossed to and fro and carried about with every wind of doctrine, by the trickery of men, in the cunning craftiness of deceitful plotting, but, speaking the truth in love, may grow up in all things into Him who is the head - Christ - from whom the whole body,

---

[134] 1 Peter 5:3
[135] W. E. Vine, An Expository Dictionary of New Testament Words; (Fleming H. Revell Company, Old Tappan, New Jersey, first printed 1940)

joined and knit together by what every joint supplies, according to the effective working by which every part does its share, causes growth of the body for the edifying of itself in love.[136]

One can readily see that all three of these words, 'elder', 'bishop' or 'overseer', and 'pastor' or 'shepherd', are used in the New Testament to refer to the same person. As Luke records Paul's message to the elders of Ephesus, as he visits them on his way back to Jerusalem, in Acts 20, he uses all three of these words to refer to the same people.

Paul called for the 'elders' of the churches in Ephesus to meet him in Miletus, where his ship stopped briefly. Then he says to them, "Therefore take heed to yourselves and to all the flock, among which the Holy Spirit has made you overseers (bishops), to shepherd (pastor) the church of God which he purchased with his own blood."[137] The apostle Peter also uses these three words to refer to the same persons.

> The elders who are among you, I exhort, I who am a fellow elder and a witness of the sufferings of Christ, and also a partaker of the glory that will be revealed: Shepherd (pastor) the flock of God, which is among you, serving as overseers (bishops), not by compulsion, but willingly, not for dishonest gain but eagerly; nor as being lords over those entrusted to you, but being examples to the flock; and when the Chief Shepherd appears, you will receive the crown of glory that does not fade away.[138]

---

[136] Ephesians 4:11-16
[137] Read Acts 20:17-31
[138] 1 Peter 5:1-4

Every pastor is an under-shepherd of the Great Shepherd, Jesus Christ. As an under-shepherd, every pastor ought to seek to model the compassionate ministry of our Lord and Savior. In John 10, Jesus uses the metaphor of the shepherd and the sheep to illustrate his relationship with his redeemed people. He says, "I am the good shepherd. The good Shepherd gives his life for the sheep."[139] He further says, "I am the good shepherd; and I know my sheep, and am known by my own."[140]

Jesus also speaks, in the same passage, of the hireling who is tending the flock. He says he is not the shepherd and does not own the sheep; so when a wolf comes, the hireling flees and abandons the sheep. The hireling flees because he does not care for the sheep; he is simply being paid to care for them. His heart is not in the task and he simply regards his work as a job for which he is being paid. It's not worth the risk of his own life to earn a few dollars. Pastor, are you a true shepherd, seeking to model the shepherding done by Jesus Himself? Or are you a hireling, who views his work as simply a job for which he is being paid?

A pastor, called to shepherd a congregation, must regard his assignment as from the Great Shepherd, Jesus Christ Himself. Jesus calls us, as pastors, to love His sheep as He loves them. Pastor, do you love the people of your flock enough that you would give your life for them? Can you say of your flock, "I know my sheep, and they know me?" If the sheep assigned to your care know that you love them to that extent, they will consider a rebuke or correction that you need to occasionally bring to

---

[139] John 10:11
[140] John 10:14

them, as an act of love from a pastor who really cares. The writer of Hebrews instructs his readers in the following way:

> Remember those who rule over you, who have spoken the word of God to you, whose faith follow, considering the outcome of their conduct. ... Obey those who rule over you, and be submissive, for they watch out for your souls, as those who must give account. Let them do so with joy and not with grief, for that would be unprofitable for you.[141]

The phrase, 'they watch out for your souls' could be rendered "they spend sleepless nights over your souls." When pastors show that kind of burden and concern for the flock over which God has made them overseers, the sheep will know their pastor truly loves them.

The Problem of Burn-Out

How does a pastor fulfill this role of pastoring his flock without burnout? Does it not seem to be such a unachievable responsibility that a pastor carries? Church congregations are partially responsible for the failure of pastors to be biblically-based servants of the Lord Jesus Christ. In the last fifty years, the expectations placed upon pastors have caused them to veer away from their essential biblical role. This is not a new problem, however, as we see the same situation occurring in the early history of the church of Jesus Christ. Luke writes, in the book of Acts, chapter 6, of the administrative challenge as the church sought to care for the physical needs of widows within the body of believers.

---

[141] Hebrews 13:7, 17

The problem arose because of a complaint by the Hellenists, or the Greek believers, against the Hebrew or Jewish believers. They felt that their Greek widows were being neglected and that the Jewish widows were being favored. Note that the problem arose as the numbers of believers were increasing rapidly.[142] As the size of the church congregation increases, the pressures upon the pastor increase. Unless the pastor, and the lay leadership of the church, take great care to maintain biblical priorities for the pastor, he will become so inundated with the administrative role, leading to neglect of his primary responsibilities. The apostles, in this early church crisis, wisely found a way to care for the problem while maintaining their biblical role in pastoring the flock.

> Therefore, brethren, seek out from among you seven men of good reputation, full of the Holy Spirit and wisdom, whom we may appoint over this business; but we will give ourselves continually to prayer and to the ministry of the word.[143]

If our evangelical churches are ever going to experience spiritual revival, it is absolutely essential that pastors be allowed to focus upon the ministry of the word of God, much prayer, and the spiritual needs of their people. Depending upon the size of the congregation, the administrative tasks must be handled by volunteer laypeople, or by additional staff. It is right for the pastor to give some general guidance to these administrative functions, as long as it does not distract from his main biblical priorities.

---

[142] Acts 6:1
[143] Acts 6:3-4

The Pastor/ Parishioner Relationship

While there are some believers who prefer to remain private and somewhat anonymous, most Christians desire to be known by their pastor. A few decades ago, it was common for the pastor of a local congregation to visit his parishioners in their homes at least once a year. These visits were not merely social calls. These were times of discipling as the pastor inquired about the spiritual lives of his flock.

Today this kind of personal care of the sheep is very rare. In fact, the larger the church becomes, the more difficult this kind of personal ministry becomes. In this technically advanced age, phone calls and emails can enable a pastor to make contact with many of his parishioners. However, these less personal methods of contact do not substitute for that personal contact that a visit provides. Even in smaller congregations today, it is rare to find a pastor who calls upon his flock in their homes. We read in Acts about the early church in the city of Jerusalem, "Continuing daily with one accord in the temple and breaking bread from house to house, they ate their food with gladness and simplicity of heart." [144] Remember that this church was already numbering over three thousand people. The 'house-to-house' ministry provided for personal teaching ministry and enabled the leaders of the church to truly know their people.

As a church grows in numbers of congregants, it is necessary to develop a culture of caring and loving the people. Obviously, it is impossible for the lead pastor to call on every believer in his home. Therefore, elders or deacons should help with this

---

[144] Acts 2:46

important ministry. One way of doing this is to assign ten to twelve family units, including single adults, to each elder or each deacon as their small flock. The elder or deacon is then responsible to provide some pastoral care for their small flock.

The minimal expectations of a deacon or elder should include: to visit each of his flock in their home at least once each year; to check on attendance patterns to be certain that his flock is in regular attendance at the worship services; to follow up by a phone call, if any of his flock are missing for more than three weeks; to follow up with frequent phone calls or emails, checking to see that all is going well; to call upon any who are hospitalized or homebound; and to report to the pastor if a pastoral call is needed in any special need situation.

The Pastor's Godly Character

It is always a tragedy when a pastor is found guilty of moral failure. The integrity and the character of the pastor is paramount. Peters tells us that an elder or pastor is to be an example to the flock.[145]

An accusation against an elder must be treated with great care. Paul tells us, "Do not receive an accusation against an elder except from two or three witnesses. Those who are sinning, rebuke in the presence of all, that the rest also may fear."[146] In other words, the truth is to be established in order to avoid false accusations that arise through gossip.

The pastor must take serious steps to assure his godly character and to prevent his fall into Satan's

---

[145] 1 Peter 5:3
[146] 1 Timothy 5:19-20

traps. This involves maintaining a close walk with Jesus Christ and keeping a check upon his thought life, his motivations, and his actions. It is so easy for a pastor to become so busy taking care of a flock that he neglects his personal walk with his Lord. Remember that Paul warns all believers, including pastors, "let him who thinks he stands take heed lest he fall."[147] Pastor, don't ever think 'it will never happen to me!' Unless you are alert to Satan's tactics, he may catch you unawares and cause you to fall at a weak moment.

Pastor, are you practicing what you preach? Your preaching will only be authentic as you are applying the truths of Scripture to your own walk.

There are three areas where Satan works overtime to lead pastors astray. They are sex, money, and pride. All believers face these same temptations; however, when Satan succeeds in getting a pastor to fail, he has succeeded in taking down a 'trophy'. The pastor who falls causes devastation that is monumentally tragic to his own life, to his family, to his congregation and to a watching world. John the apostle exhorts all believers:

> Do not love the world or the things in the world. If anyone loves the world, the love of the father is not in him. For all that is in the world - the lust of the flesh, the lust of the eyes, and the pride of life - is not of the father, but is of the world. And the world is passing away, and the lust of it; but he who does the will of God abides forever.[148]

Someone has said that it is possible to translate this, "stop loving the world or the things in the world."

---

[147] 1 Corinthians 10:12
[148] 1 John 2:15-17

John is talking about a constant problem that the believer needs to deal with in his life. It is so easy to be infatuated with the things of the world system. Paul exhorts us:

> If then you were raised with Christ, seek those things which are above, where Christ is, sitting at the right hand of God. Set your mind on things above, not on things on the earth. For you died, and your life is hidden with Christ in God. When Christ, who is our life appears, then you also will appear with him in glory.

> Therefore, put to death your members which are on the earth: fornication, uncleanness, passion, evil desire, and covetousness, which is idolatry. Because of these things the wrath of God is coming upon the sons of disobedience, in which you yourselves once walked when you lived in them. But now you yourselves are to put off all these: anger, wrath, malice, blasphemy, filthy language out of your mouth. Do not lie to one another, since you have put off the old man with his deeds, and have put on the new man who is renewed in knowledge, according to the image of Him who created him . . .

> Therefore, as the elect of God, holy and beloved, put on tender mercies, kindness, humility, meekness, long suffering; bearing with one another, and forgiving one another, if anyone has a complaint against another; even as Christ forgave you, you also must do. But above all these things put on love, which is the bond of perfection.[149]

---

[149] Colossians 3:1-14

The Scriptures teach that all sin starts in the mind.[150]. It is therefore imperative that a pastor keeps a constant guard upon his thought life. Falling into sexual sin happens when one allows his mind to be filled with lustful thoughts. No person can prevent a lustful thought from entering his mind, but he can eliminate it immediately. Remember that Jesus said: "Whoever looks at a woman to lust for her has already committed adultery with her in his heart."[151] As someone said, "You cannot prevent a bird from landing on your head, but you can prevent it from building a nest in your hair!" You must bring "every thought into captivity"[152] if you are to experience victory over the lust of the flesh.

Every church and every pastor ought to adopt a clear policy regarding counseling, especially when counseling those of the opposite sex. Such a policy is a protection for the pastor or other staff when counseling, as well as for the counselee. This policy should at least include the following: No one will counsel a person of the opposite sex in any room that does not have windows that allow for visibility; No one will counsel a person of the opposite sex when you are alone in the building; Counseling sessions will not exceed forty-five minutes in length, especially when counseling the opposite sex.

A pastor's counseling sessions should never exceed two or three sessions. Dr. Robert Smith, a very godly professor at Bethel Theological College and Seminary during my seminary days, believed that if you could not help a person through counseling from the Scriptures in one, two, or three sessions at the most, you will never be able to help that person.

---

[150] James 1:13-14
[151] Matthew 5:28
[152] 2 Corinthians: 10 3-6

Besides, the counseling ministry of a pastor is often counterproductive. It is very time-consuming, taking away from the biblical priorities of a pastor.

When a pastor spends extensive time in counseling, that parishioner often ends up going to another congregation, because he or she feels that the pastor knows too much about his or her intimate lives. Many pastors who fall into sexual sin will testify that it all began with counseling a person of the opposite sex.

Pastors and pastors' wives need to give priority to their marriage and their family life. If there is a strained relationship between a pastor and his wife, and if there is no physical intimacy between them, they are putting each other in a very dangerous situation. If this is the case in your life, pastor, do not allow the situation to continue – get help for your marriage. Satan knows that you are vulnerable and the costs of falling are too great and too devastating.

How about the area of money and prosperity? Greed and covetousness are huge obstacles to victory when they are allowed to prowl unchecked in your life. It is not money, but rather the love of money, that is sinful. As Paul the apostle writes to young pastor Timothy, he says:

> Now godliness with contentment is great gain. For we brought nothing into this world, and it is certain we can carry nothing out. And having food and clothing, with these we shall be content. But those who desire to be rich fall into a temptation and a snare, and into many foolish and harmful lusts which drown men in destruction and perdition. For the love of money is a root of all kinds of evil, for

which some have strayed from the faith in their greediness, and pierced themselves through with many sorrows.

But you, O man of God, believe these things, and pursue righteousness, godliness, faith, love, patience, gentleness. Fight the good fight of faith, lay hold on eternal life, to which you are also called and have confessed the good confession in the presence of many witnesses.[153]

Another problem area for pastors is that of pride and self-seeking. When the Lord blesses the pastor's work and the church is growing in numbers, it is easy to begin taking credit for what is happening. Remember, if people are being saved and Christians are being discipled, it is not because you are such a great pastor. It is because the Lord Jesus has called you, equipped you and is using you as an instrument in His hand. Therefore humble yourself and give all the glory to God. He alone is worthy of praise and glory!

Many are the pastors who are seeking for advancement. They desire a bigger church or an influential position amongst their peers. This is the way of the world! Serve with contentment where the Lord has placed you. Fulfill your ministry under the power and direction of the Holy Spirit of God. If God wants you to serve in a larger capacity, He will take care of opening the door before you. You do not need to push yourself forward or seek to manipulate the circumstances in your efforts to open the door.

Experiencing Victory in Jesus

---

[153] 1 Timothy 6:6-12

The Scriptures are replete with commands that we should flee from these traps. "Flee from idolatry."[154] "Flee sexual immorality."[155] "Flee from these things (greed and the desire and love of money)."[156] "Flee youthful lusts."[157] To flee means to put distance between you and that from which you are fleeing. Don't hang around and listen to Satan until you fall into his trap, ending up in full-blown sin. Keep short accounts with the Lord Jesus and forsake all appearance of evil.

There is a way to victory over sin. In Romans 6, the apostle Paul teaches us that because we are in Christ, we are no longer slaves to sin.[158] We are to continually give ourselves to be slaves of righteousness and godliness. When we resist Satan, he will flee from us.[159]

'Victory in Jesus' must become more than a song that we sing. It must be our experience every day and every moment of our lives. Claim the promise of the Lord given through the apostle Paul in   1 Corinthians 10:13,

> No temptation has overtaken you except such as is common to man; but God is faithful, who will not allow you to be tempted beyond what you are able, but with the temptation will also make the way of escape, that you may be able to bear it.

Every pastor ought to have an accountability partner in ministry! When two likeminded pastors hold

---

[154] 1 Corinthians 10:14
[155] 1 Corinthians 6:18
[156] 1 Timothy 6:11
[157] 2 Timothy 2:22
[158] Read Romans 6:4-22
[159] James 4:7

each other accountable, both are far more likely to know victory in their walk with the Lord. However, each must honestly and openly answer to each other. Meet for an accountability session at least once a month. Ask each other the following questions and make certain that each is answering honestly.

1.   How is your devotional time with the Lord going? What has the Lord shown you specifically that is enabling you to grow in your relationship with him?

2.   Are you struggling with any temptations that you have faced since we last met? Have you stayed away from pornography on the Internet, or any other source? Are you keeping your mind in captivity to Jesus Christ?

3.   Are you content with what you have been given by the Lord? Since we last met, have you allowed any lust for money, sex, higher position or greater power?

4.   Is there any sin in your life right now that you have not openly dealt with before the Lord? To the best of your knowledge, are you clean before the Lord?

5.   Is there anything that the Holy Spirit is putting His finger upon in your life that you have not openly shared with me today? Are you hiding anything from me?

When a pastor will develop such a relationship with another pastor he can trust with the most intimate details of his life, this relationship will go a long way to maintaining his godly integrity as a pastor. They need to pray daily for each other. Call each other frequently, and keep each other accountable before God.

I urge you, pastor, to renew your call to biblical pastoring. Feed your flock, preach the whole counsel of God, love your sheep and lead them in ways everlasting! Trust the Lord to use His word as it goes forth faithfully from your heart and from your mouth. Leave the results to the Lord; He alone gives the increase.[160]

---

[160] Read 1 Corinthians 3:6-7

Chapter 7

True Gospel or Another Gospel

Evangelism scares most Christians. Images enter their minds of believers who buttonhole people and won't let them go, until they have shared the gospel with them. Most believers settle with living in a good way and leaving the sharing of the gospel message to the professionals, the pastors and evangelists like Billy Graham. J. Mack Stiles says:

> If I were in jail for evangelism, I'm pretty sure that I would be asking friends to pray that God would "get me out!" But the imprisoned Paul's prayer requests were for boldness and clarity with the gospel (Ephesians 6:19; Colossians 4:3-4). [161]

Whether in chains, watched by Roman guard, or free to travel, Paul was constantly witnessing by sharing the gospel of the Lord Jesus Christ. When in prison he took the opportunity to be a witness to Caesar's household and to the guards who watched him day and night. As he writes to the church at Philippi, he says this:

> But I want you to know, brethren, that the things which happened to me have actually turned out for the furtherance of the gospel, so that it has become evident to the whole palace guard, and to all the rest, that my chains are in Christ; and most of the brethren in the Lord, having become confident by my chains, are

---

[161] Evangelism, How the Whole Church Speaks of Jesus; J. Mack Stiles, (Crossway, Wheaton, Illinois), 2014, page 106

much more bold to speak the word without fear.[162]

About forty years ago, 'friendship evangelism' was the big push. I have no quarrel with friendship evangelism for we, as believers in Christ, ought to be building bridges of friendship with all of our neighbors and our coworkers. However, a breakdown occurs in the process of befriending our neighbors. Most of us end up forever building bridges while neglecting to share the good news of the gospel message. Most of us fail at the point of having courage to tell our new friends about our Savior. We must remember that they will never be saved merely by our sincere friendship and observing our good living. They must hear the gospel message.

J. Mack Stiles writes about developing a culture of evangelism in every local church. His book is an excellent read. It is one of a series of books called, "Nine Marks - Building Healthy Churches". We must develop a culture of evangelism in the congregation. There is no one right way of evangelizing. We must always be sowing the seed of the word of God in the lives of others.

A Christian who was active in evangelism was criticized by another Christian, saying, "I don't like the way you do evangelism!" So the Christian responded, "how do you do evangelism?" The critical Christian responded, "I don't do evangelism!" The evangelistic Christian responded, "Well, I like the way I am doing evangelism better than the way you are not doing evangelism!"

What is the Gospel?

---

[162] Philippians 1:12-14

In developing a culture of evangelism we must be crystal clear about what the gospel really is. As Paul indicates in his letter to the Galatians, there are many false 'gospels' being preached. Paul warns about a false or perverted gospel.

> I marvel that you are turning away so soon from him who called you in the grace of Christ, to a different gospel, which is not another; but there are some who trouble you and want to pervert the gospel of Christ. But even if we, or an angel from heaven, preach any other gospel to you than what we have preached to you, let him be accursed. As we have said before, so now I say again, if anyone preaches any other gospel to you than what you have received, let him be accursed. For do I now persuade men, or God? Or do I seek to please men? For if I still pleased men, I would not be a bondservant of Christ.[163]

The false gospel to which Paul was referring was the gospel being preached by the Judaizers who were insisting upon adding circumcision as a requirement for salvation. Paul resisted this tenaciously because this would have added human works to grace as a requirement for salvation. Whenever we add anything to repentance and faith we are no longer preaching a gospel of God's grace. We are saved by grace alone in Christ alone by faith alone.

The False Gospel of Easy-Believism

One form of a false gospel that is prevalent today is what many have called "easy-believism". After Paul

---

[163] Galatians 1:6-10

and Silas had been imprisoned at Philippi, the jailer who was shaken by the earthquake that opened up the jail cells, asks, "What must I do to be saved?" The apostle Paul responded: "Believe on the Lord Jesus Christ, and you will be saved, you and your household."[164]

In the context of Jesus' conversation with Nicodemus about the necessity of a new birth, we find Christ's statement which some have called "the gospel in a nutshell".

> For God so loved the world that He gave His only begotten Son, that whoever believes in Him should not perish but have everlasting life. For God did not send his Son into the world to condemn the world, but that the world through Him might be saved. He who believes in Him is not condemned; but he who does not believe is condemned already, because he has not believed in the name of the only begotten Son of God.[165]

What does it mean to believe in the Lord Jesus Christ? Some quickly respond that to believe means that you believe Jesus Christ died for your sin, was raised again from the dead, and that He will forgive your sins. This leads to defining 'believe' as merely an intellectual assent to some true facts about Jesus Christ. Believe means much more than an intellectual assent. This definition of believe has resulted in many stillborn "believers" who are members of our evangelical churches. They believe they have fire insurance against going to hell when they die. However, they are just as lost and just as much a child of God's wrath as they were before they embraced this false idea of faith.

---

[164] Acts 16:30-31
[165] John 3:16-18

David Platt, in his books, challenges us to rethink this kind of gospel that has been so widely accepted in the evangelical world. He says that the gospel involves dying to our lives and totally surrendering in willingness to die for Jesus sake. He uses the example of four fishermen, called by Jesus to leave their fishing business and to follow Him. He says that each of these fishermen paid a costly ultimate price as they were put to death for their faith in Jesus Christ. It is true that at the time of their call to follow Jesus, they gave up everything in order to be obedient to Christ. They left their boats, their fishing nets, their father and their way of life. However, the disciples struggled many times in following Jesus. They grew in their faith and their commitment as they walked with Jesus. Following His resurrection they were transformed and lived out the rest of their lives with a total willingness to give their lives for Jesus sake.

We must not make the mistake of equating the salvation experience to the sanctification process yet faced by a baby Christian. Having said this, it is well worth our time to consider the challenge that David Platt gives us. He says in his book, 'Radical':

> Suddenly contemporary Christianity sales pitches don't seem adequate anymore. Asked Jesus to come into your heart. Invite Jesus to come into your life. Pray this prayer, sign this card, walk down this aisle, and accept Jesus as your personal Savior. Our attempt to reduce this gospel to a shrink-wrapped presentation that persuades someone to say or pray the right things back to us no longer seems appropriate.

That is why none of these man-made catch-phrases are in the Bible. You will not find a verse in Scripture where people are told to "bow your heads, close your eyes, and repeat after me." You will not find a place where a superstitious sinner's prayer is even mentioned. And you will not find an emphasis on accepting Jesus. We have taken the infinitely glorious Son of God, who endure the infinitely terrible wrath of God and who now reigns as the infinitely worthy Lord of all, and we have reduced him to a poor, puny Savior, who is just begging for us to accept him.[166]

David Platt continues in his second book, Follow Me:

Churches are filled with supposed Christians who seem content to have a casual association with Christ, while giving nominal adherence to Christianity. Scores of men, women, and children have been told that becoming a follower of Jesus simply involves acknowledging certain facts or saying certain words. But this is not true. Disciples like Peter, Andrew, James, John, and Ayaan[167] show us that the call to follow Jesus is not simply an invitation to pray a prayer; it's a summons to lose our lives.

---

[166] David Platt, Radical, IBID, pages 36-37

[167] Ayan is a Muslim woman, whom David Platt led to an experience of salvation. He uses her as an example of one who paid a very costly price in accepting Christ as her Savior and Lord. As he says in his book, for her faith meant "literally to die to her life. To die to her family. To die to her friends. To die to her future. And in dying, to live. To live in Jesus."

Why, then, would we think that becoming a Christian means anything less for us? And why would we not want to die to ourselves in order to live in Christ? Yes, there is a cost that accompanies stepping out of casual, comfortable, cultural Christianity, but it is worth it. More aptly put, He is worth it. Jesus is worthy of far more than intellectual belief, and there is so much more to following him than monotonous spirituality. There is indescribable joy to be found, deep satisfaction to be felt, and eternal purpose to be fulfilled in dying to ourselves and living for him.[168]

So, what does it mean to believe in Jesus Christ?

It is obvious that Jesus Christ meant more than mental assent when he told people to believe in Him and receive Him. As you read the Gospels, Jesus is more interested in followers who are willing to abandon all for His sake. To believe in Him was to embrace Him with your heart and allow Him to be the Master of your life. It meant that you were committed to learning to obediently follow Him out of gratitude for His grace in saving you from your sin. As David Platt correctly reminds us: "surely this gospel evokes unconditional surrender of all that we are and all that we have to all that He is."[169]

It doesn't take much of a man to become a Christian but it takes all there is of him. True saving faith involves a person's entire being, mind, heart and soul. True saving faith will always bring change in a

---

[168] David Platt, Follow Me, (Tyndale House publishers, Carol Stream, Illinois) 2013; pages 3-4
[169] David Platt, Radical, IBID, page 37

person's lifestyle. If there is no evidence of a changed life after one has made a profession of faith in Jesus Christ, then we know that person is not truly saved. We are not saved by our works, but we are saved "unto good works which God has ordained that we should walk in them."[170]

The epistle of 1 John was written that we might know for sure that we possess eternal life.[171] The apostle John clearly states that anyone who says he believes in Jesus Christ, who continues on in the same sinful patterns of life, is not truly born from above, but continues to be a child of the devil. A changed life is the fruit produced by genuine saving faith. Good works are not the means of salvation, but the result of salvation produced by the Holy Spirit in your life.

> Whoever abides in Him does not sin. Whoever sins has neither seen Him nor known Him. Little children, let no one deceive you. He who practices righteousness is righteous, just as He is righteous. He who sins is of the devil, for the devil has sinned, from the beginning. For this purpose the Son of God was manifested, that He might destroy the works of the devil. Whoever has been born of God does not sin, for His seed remains in him; and he cannot sin, because he has been born of God. In this the children of God and the children of the devil are manifest: who ever does not practice righteousness is not of God, nor is he who does not love his brother.[172]

---

[170] Ephesians 2:10
[171] Read 1 John 5:12-13
[172] 1 John 3:6-10

John does not refer here to the Christian who occasionally sins. Rather, the form of the verbs used by John, indicate continual action of sinning. When Jesus Christ truly enters into a person's life, and the Holy Spirit produces the new birth, that person desires to follow the Lord Jesus Christ and to be obedient to Him. This is what Paul means in 2 Corinthians 5:17, when he teaches that "If anyone is in Christ, he is a new creation; old things have passed away; behold, all things have become new."

In Romans 10:9-10, Paul shows that believing in Jesus Christ involves the mind and the heart. To believe means giving up ruling your own life and allowing Jesus Christ to rule your life. "If you confess with your mouth the Lord Jesus and believe in your heart that God has raised Him from the dead, you will be saved. For with the heart one believes unto righteousness, and with the mouth confession is made unto salvation." Confessing with your mouth the Lord Jesus means owning Him as your Lord and Master.

A word of caution is in order here. To allow Jesus Christ to be Lord of one's life, as one yields his life to Him and trusts Him as Savior, does not mean that he will live a perfect life in the future. The new believer has no idea, at this point of his salvation experience, what all the implications of Christ's Lordship mean. He will discover these as he walks in faith with Jesus Christ. He will grow in his submission to Christ as Lord. Allowing Christ to be Lord in his life is an attitude of submitting to Him because of what He has done for him in providing his salvation.

A False Gospel without Repentance

Another form of a false gospel leaves out the matter of repentance. Jesus Himself preached repentance. Matthew 4:17 says, "From that time Jesus began to preach and to say, 'repent, for the kingdom of heaven is at hand.'" The gospel of Mark makes it very clear that Jesus preached repentance and belief in the gospel.[173]

Jesus stated unequivocally that repentance is necessary in order to escape God's judgment upon our sin and in order to escape hell.

> There were present at that season some who told Him about the Galileans whose blood Pilate had mingled with their sacrifices. And Jesus answered and said to them, "Do you suppose that these Galileans were worse sinners than all other Galileans, because they suffered such things? I tell you, no; but unless you repent you will all likewise perish.
>
> Or those eighteen on whom the tower in Siloam fell and killed them, do you think that they were worse sinners than all other men who dwelt in Jerusalem? I tell you, no; but unless you repent you will all likewise perish."[174]

After His resurrection Jesus conversed with two disciples as they walked the road to Emmaus. They invited Him to join them for a meal. While Jesus broke bread with them, their eyes were opened to see that their guest really was Jesus who had been raised from the dead. Jesus then vanished from their sight.[175]

---

[173] Mark 1:14-15
[174] Luke 13:1-5
[175] Luke 24:13-31

Returning to Jerusalem, the two who experienced the presence of the resurrected Lord, sought out the place where the eleven disciples and others were gathered. As they were sharing their experiences, Jesus suddenly appeared in their midst. They were all terrified and frightened. Jesus reassured them and gave them proof through the observance of His wounds that He indeed had risen from the dead. In some of Jesus' final words which He spoke on this occasion, He commissioned His disciples to preach "repentance and remission of sins" to all nations, beginning in Jerusalem.[176]

When have you last heard a message about repentance in an evangelical church? When the gospel is preached, the necessity of repentance is seldom included. Repentance is the lost ingredient of the gospel. What a tragedy, in the light of the fact that Jesus himself commissioned us to preach repentance to all people! A person cannot turn to Jesus Christ without turning away from his sin.

Jesus says in Luke 15:7 that there is "more joy in heaven over one sinner who repents than over ninety nine just persons who need no repentance." Peter, while preaching on the day of Pentecost (when the Holy Spirit was poured out upon believers) in Acts 2:38, says, "Repent, and let every one of you be baptized in the name of Jesus Christ for the remission of sins; and you shall receive the gift of the Holy Spirit." Peter also writes in 2 Peter 3:9: "The Lord is not slack concerning His promise, as some count slackness, but is longsuffering toward us, not willing that any should perish but that all should come to repentance."

---

[176] Luke 24:46-49

There is a common misunderstanding about the nature of repentance. Most people define repentance as "turning away from one's sin." Certainly this is involved. Repent, however, basically means 'to change the mind.' It is not a matter of reforming your way of life for this would be your own self effort, your own good works. This does not bring salvation as we have already seen.

Repentance means a change of one's thinking that is brought about by the Holy Spirit of God using the word of God which is God's truth. Note how Paul, the apostle, describes it as he is instructing
Timothy about the work of the servant of God in 2 Timothy 2:24 -26.

> And a servant of the Lord must not quarrel but be gentle to all, able to teach, patient, in humility correcting those who are in opposition, if God perhaps will grant them repentance, so that they may know the truth, and that they may come to their senses and escape the snare of the devil, having been taken captive by him to do his will.

Repentance means coming to your spiritual senses as your thinking is changed by the Holy Spirit as He uses the truth of God's word in your life. Let's examine the changes in your thinking that take place when the Holy Spirit brings about repentance in your life.

You think differently about God. You see God as holy and righteous in all His ways. He is perfect in every way and cannot tolerate any taint of sin. You no longer see God as a harsh, vindictive God who delights in punishing sinners; rather, you see Him as the God who loves you so much that He has given his own Son as a sacrifice for your sin.

You think differently about your own sin. Instead of seeing yourself as good enough to get to heaven on your own merit, you see yourself as a sinner. You see yourself as deserving of God's judgment and punishment. You begin to see how sinful you are in your selfish ways. As one author has put it, "Too many think lightly of sin, and therefore think lightly of the Savior. He who has stood before God, convicted and condemned, with the rope about his neck, is the man to weep for joy when he is pardoned, to hate evil which is forgiven him, and to live to the honor of the Redeemer by whose blood he has been cleansed."[177]

You think differently about Jesus Christ. You now see Him as God, the Son, who suffered and died for you that He might rescue you from God's wrath upon your sin. You see Him as the loving Savior who gave Himself that you might have eternal life.

The apostle Paul distinguishes between being sorry and being repentant. Through one of his letters to the Corinthian church, he had caused them sorrow. As he writes in 2 Corinthians, he talks about two kinds of sorrow, godly sorrow and worldly sorrow. Godly sorrow leads to repentance while worldly sorrow leads to death.[178] Do not confuse being sorry for your sin as being repentant. It is godly sorrow that brings true repentance.

Martyn Lloyd-Jones describes repentance in this way:

> Repentance means that you realize that you are a guilty, vile sinner in the presence of

[177] Arnold Dallimore, Spurgeon, (Banner of Truth Trust, Carlisle, Pennsylvania), 1985; Page 14
[178] 2 Corinthians 7:8-11

God, that you deserve the wrath and punishment of God, that you are hell-bound. It means that you begin to realize that this thing called sin is in you, that you long to get rid of it, and that you turn your back on it in every shape and form . . . That is repentance. [179]

When we truly are brought by the Holy Spirit to godly repentance, we see ourselves honestly in the light of God's holiness and righteousness. The modern perspective is that we as human beings should think positively about ourselves rather than seeing ourselves as helpless sinners. While this "I'm OK, you're OK!" stroking of our egos may result in some progress in our cultural setting, it interferes in our spiritual relationship with God. It prevents us from seeing our desperate need of being rescued from our spiritual deadness by the Lord Jesus Christ. Mac Brunson expresses it in this way:

Lowliness of spirit, means seeing ourselves honestly, seeing ourselves as wretched, miserable creatures who have nothing to offer God, but outstretched empty hands - hands that need to be filled with His goodness and righteousness.

I realize that this is not a popular view in some Christian circles. There is a brand of Christianity today that says it is unhealthy for us to think of ourselves as sinners. The great reformers such as Martin Luther, Ulrich Zwingli, John Knox, and others did not think this way, nor did the "Pre-Reformation" reformers such as John Huss. The great

[179] Martin Lloyd-Jones, Sermon on the Mount, (Eerdman's Publishing Company, Grand Rapids, Michigan), 1972; Page 248

preachers of history, such as Charles Simeon, John Newton, Charles Wesley, George Whitfield, D. L. Moody, Charles Spurgeon, and a host of others recognize that all of us are sinners. But much of contemporary Christianity has been diluted by pop psychology and infiltrated by a self-centeredness that rejects the idea of our fallen nature.[180]

The Altar Call

The altar call came to be a common practice as frontier evangelists preached the gospel to crowds of people. One fails to find such a practice in the New Testament. Baptism in the New Testament was the means of declaring one's faith in the Lord Jesus Christ. When a person hears the gospel and responds by placing his faith in the Lord Jesus Christ, his first declaration publicly of his faith and trust in Jesus Christ is to submit to being baptized (immersed) in water. Immersion in water clearly pictures the gospel message as the person declares "I have accepted the death, burial, and resurrection of Jesus Christ, for salvation from my sin." When the believer is lowered into the water, it pictures his identification with the death of Jesus Christ. Under the water, the picture is of burial with Jesus Christ. When he is raised from the water, it pictures his resurrection in Jesus Christ to a brand-new life given to him by the Holy Spirit of God.[181]

---

[180] The God You've Been Searching For, Mac Brunson (Moody publishers, Chicago, Illinois, 1957), page 60

[181] A note to those who define baptism differently: I have stated how I see baptism as taught in the New Testament. If you are of a different persuasion, I leave it to you to square your belief with Scripture. Seeing baptism as the means of salvation, rather than the means of declaring one's faith, is also a false form of the gospel.

I do not see the altar call as necessarily a wrong method. However, an altar call needs to be carefully done in order to avoid false professions that do nothing more than provide an evangelist or a pastor with additional statistics, and worst of all, may give a false assurance of salvation. Mere profession of faith in Christ, without true faith given by the Holy Spirit to a seeking heart, does not bring the new birth.

Recently I attended a huge Christmas celebration and production at a large church. It was an extravaganza, done professionally with all the glitz of modern technology. At the intermission the pastor rose to speak briefly to the congregation. He shared with us that their church had been doing such a Christmas presentation for thirty two years and that they plan to continue it indefinitely. He gave his brief presentation of the gospel. Then he asked all of us to bow our heads in prayer. He asked people to repeat a prayer after him, and asked that they should pray out loud where they were seated. There were many people who did pray that prayer audibly. The pastor then assured them that because they had prayed the sinner's prayer, they were on their way to heaven. Really?

J. Mack Stiles says this about altar calls:

> Many people have responded to altar-calls over the decades. But for all who have been genuinely converted when they responded, there have been many more who merely came to the front of the church building out of some other compulsion . . . Most important, even though people come to Jesus through various means, the Bible never uses results to guide or justify evangelistic practice.

156

So when we set out to practice evangelism, we must start with biblical foundations. We must look to these to shape, guard, and inform how we share our faith rather than starting by looking for a way to gain maximum impact. We must be very careful to conform our evangelistic practice to the Bible, because this honors God.

Sadly, what often informs our evangelistic practices is the world - perhaps the business world or the self-help section in the bookstore - rather than the Scriptures. Satan plays to our desire for results by offering a bigger TV ministry or financial profit. He even tempts us with seemingly good-hearted desires such as an expanded membership or the undying belief that if a child prays a sinner's prayer, he or she has become a committed believer, regardless of how he or she lives. In all this, people trade biblical principles for worldly desires, and our evangelistic practices get twisted.[182]

Invitations, or altar calls, are often done in such a way that it requires nothing of the responder. "If you prayed that prayer, with no one looking around, just slip up your hand quickly and put it down again, indicating to me that you have made that decision." Why do we do this? Did not Jesus say, "Whoever is ashamed of Me and My words, of him the Son of Man will be ashamed when He comes in His own glory, and in His Father's and of the holy angels."[183]

J. Mack Stiles gives us this cogent advice:

---

[182] J. Mack Stiles, IBID, Pages 24-25
[183] Luke 9:26

If I could, I would love to go back in time and teach the church in Memphis (the church he used to pastor) what evangelism really is. I would warn that there is much sickness in the church worldwide because of churches calling something evangelism when it is not. "Please," I would beg, "when you teach, don't teach people about how to behave during an invitation. Teach clearly what the gospel is and what is required of a person to turn to Christ."

I would urge the church to aim to persuade, but to persuade without manipulation. I would encourage them not to exclude what is hard about the Christian life, however tempting that may be; not to confuse human response for a move of the Spirit; and not to lie about results. "And please," I would say, "be wary of calling people Christians without some evidence that they are truly converted followers."

. . . If we are honest, we have to say that we face the same temptation to sacrifice biblical principles for results and "success." As I look around, I don't see that much has changed besides the form in which we practice unbiblical evangelism. The gospel often remains untaught, and un-biblical words water down the poignant true meaning of sin, death, and hell, or confuse those who are genuinely seeking truth.[184]

---

[184] J. Mack Stiles, IBID, Pages 27-28

Are we guilty of trivializing the grace of God? The grace of God is God doing for us that which we cannot do for ourselves, and that which we do not deserve. However, God's grace is not available to anyone when there is no repentance and when one does not believe in Jesus Christ with his heart and mind. Grace is not permissiveness; that is, grace does not come to one who plans to continue on in his old life. Grace does not treat sin casually. The one who receives God's grace, forgiving and cleansing him from his sin, granting to him the gift of eternal life, is the one who has come to the foot of the cross. He is the one who recognizes that his redemption and forgiveness has been bought at tremendous cost to Jesus Christ.

It is time for us to seriously re-examine our methods of evangelism. It is time to re-establish the true gospel. For the sake of the members of our evangelical churches who are not yet born again, let's cease giving false assurance when there is no biblical evidence of any true salvation.

Chapter 8

Our Marching Orders

As we examine the average local evangelical church, how seriously does it take the Great Commission given to us by the Lord of the church? Is your church guilty of trivializing the mission of the church? Does our myopic vision only view our local community? Are we able to view the whole world as our responsibility? Is your church involved in just maintenance or is your church on mission to reach all people with the gospel of Jesus Christ? Is your church involved in some plan to help fulfill the commission of sharing the gospel with the world?

The Great Commission, given by the Lord Jesus Himself, is the marching order for the church of Jesus Christ. Every local church and every believer in the church must take seriously the commission given to us by Christ.

David Platt, in the introduction to his second book, Follow Me, says:

> The issue is not about having a small church or a big one. It is about how to keep the great commission at the forefront of every believer's mind. It is about helping the church go beyond "come and listen." to "go and tell." It is about believers experiencing real life and about the church of Jesus shining brightly.[185]

In far too many churches professing believers have become spectators rather than laborers in the

---

[185] David Platt, Follow Me (Tyndale House Publishers, Carol Stream, Illinois, 2013) page XII

harvest fields. We have lost our vision of the harvest or perhaps have never had a vision of the harvest field. As the disciples returned from purchasing food in the town of Sychar, they marveled that Jesus was talking with a woman. It seemed even stranger to them that he was talking with a Samaritan woman. As Jesus sought to instill in his disciples a vision for lost people, he said to them:

> My food, is to do the will of Him who sent Me, and to finish His work. Do you not say, 'There are still four months and then comes the harvest?' Behold, I say to you, lift up your eyes and look at the fields, for they are already white for harvest. And he who reaps receives wages, and gathers fruit for eternal life, that both he who sows and he who reaps may rejoice together. For in this the saying is true: 'one sows and another reaps.' I sent you to reap that for which you have not labored; others have labored, and you have entered into their labors.[186]

The harvest field is the entire world! It has always been God's intention and desire that all nations will praise His name. When God called Abraham to leave his home in Ur of the Chaldees, and to journey to a land that he would show him, He promised him, "In you all the families of the earth shall be blessed."[187] The Lord Jesus came to our world to die for the sins of all people, not just for the Jews, or any other select group of people. The apostle John reminds us, "For God so loved the world that He gave His only begotten Son, that

---

[186] John 4:34-38
[187] Genesis 12:3

whoever believes in Him, should not perish but have everlasting life."[188]

The apostle John is given insight into the eternal realm as God is about to bring the world, as we know it, to a conclusion. He hears a new song being sung by the four living creatures and the twenty four elders as they worship the Lamb of God. They sing

> You are worthy to take the scroll, and to open its seals, for You were slain, and have redeemed us to God by your blood out of every tribe and tongue and people and nation, and have made us kings and priests to our God, and we shall reign on the earth.[189]

When God's people are all gathered together in the presence of our Savior, there will be a worldwide representation from "every tribe and tongue and people and nation."

We who claim the name of Jesus Christ, in the Western world, are desperately in need of revival in our lives. Until we catch the vision of a lost world on its way to a Christless eternity in the fires of hell, we will continue to play trivia games. As the late Dr. S. M. Lockridge used to say, "Nothing is going to happen through you until something happens to you!"

Understanding the Great Commission

Just before Jesus ascended to the Father in heaven He commissioned all of His followers to be witnesses for Him, beginning in Jerusalem, and then

---

[188] John 3:16
[189] Revelation 5:9-10

spreading throughout Judea, and Samaria, and ultimately to the ends of the earth.[190]

In all three of the synoptic Gospels, the Great Commission appears in some form.[191] Here is Matthew's version of our Lord's commission.

> And Jesus came and spoke to them, saying, All authority has been given to Me in heaven and on earth. Go therefore and make disciples of all nations, baptizing them in the name of the Father and of the Son and of the Holy Spirit, teaching them to observe all things that I have commanded you; and lo, I am with you always, even to the end of the age. Amen.

The main verb in the Great Commission is 'make disciples'. All the other verb forms are participles relating to the main verb. Many, many sermons have been preached on the Great Commission that tell us to go to the far reaches of the world with the gospel message. While this is certainly a true message, and it is included in the Great Commission, it is not the main command found in Christ's assignment to us. Every believer in Jesus Christ is to be involved in making disciples or followers of Jesus. Not all of us are called to go to foreign lands to share the gospel. However, all of us are called to be 'making disciples' as we are living our daily lives in this world.

None of us is excused from the Great Commission. For every believer, every follower of Jesus Christ, our career is to make disciples of Jesus Christ. Whatever our occupation may be, it is really only a means of paying expenses. Our occupation is to be carried out in such a way that shows us to be

---

[190] Acts 1:8
[191] Matthew 28:18-20; Mark 16:15; Luke 24:46-48

followers of Jesus Christ by seeking to persuade others to be followers of Jesus. As each believer accepts his responsibility to be a witness for his master, the Lord Jesus Christ, he will do all he can to fulfill the Great Commission. He will witness by the life he lives and by the gospel he shares wherever he happens to be living. He will also be a prayer warrior for the advancement of the gospel around the world. In addition, he will give as much as he possibly can to financially support missions around the world.

In our western world evangelical churches, our focus upon measuring success by numbers has led us to count decisions rather than to make disciples. In many of our churches, when someone prays the prayer to accept Jesus Christ, we assume that our mission is complete. Suppose the person is sincere and truly understands the gospel, is that person committed to being a disciple of Jesus Christ?

What is a Disciple?

The word "disciple" literally means "a learner" who is seeking to follow his teacher. According to Vine's Expository Dictionary of New Testament Words, "a disciple is not only a pupil, but an adherent; hence they are spoken of as imitators of their teacher."[192] . Therefore, the goal of the Great Commission is to make disciples or followers of Jesus Christ. While this certainly involves the beginning steps of repentance and placing one's faith or trust in Jesus Christ, it does not end there. The Great Commission clearly states that the one who trusts Jesus Christ as Savior will also commit himself to becoming a follower of Jesus Christ. He must publicly proclaim

[192] An Expository Dictionary of the New Testament Words, W. E. Vine (Fleming H. Revell Company, Old Tappan, New Jersey, 1940) page 316

his faith by being baptized in the name of the triune God. From that time on, his goal will be learning to follow obediently in the steps of His Master, Jesus Christ.

Jesus defined a disciple as one, who when perfectly trained, is just like his teacher.[193] As the apostle Paul assures us that God is working all things together for our good, he reminds us that God is seeking to conform us to the image of Jesus Christ.[194] One of the characteristics of a disciple is that he will abide in God's word.[195] To abide in God's word means that a disciple will be a student of God's word, seeking not only to know God's word intellectually, but to practically obey God's word in his daily life.

Jesus gives another characteristic of a true disciple in John 13:34-35. "A new commandment I give to you, that you love one another; as I have loved you, that you also love one another. By this all will know that you are My disciples, if you have love for one another." To love one another is to sacrifice ourselves for the good of our brothers and sisters in Christ, and for the benefit of non-believers around us.

The apostle John further defines this love in 1 John 3:16-18:

> By this we know love, because He laid down His life for us. And we also ought to lay down our lives for the brethren. But whoever has this world's goods, and sees his brother in need, and shuts up his heart from him, how does the love of God abide in him? My little

---

[193] Luke 6:40
[194] Romans 8:28-29
[195] John 8:31-32

children, let us not love in word or in tongue, but in deed and in truth.

According to Jesus, the disciple is one who bears much fruit.[196] Certainly this involves producing the fruit of the Spirit in our lives, which is the opposite of the evil workings of our old sinful nature.[197] Additionally, a true disciple must also become a disciple maker. He must also take up his place in seeking to fulfill the Great Commission.

As you read through the Gospels, you will find Jesus constantly challenging people to become true disciples who are seeking to live their daily lives for the sake of His kingdom. Jesus teaches us that following Him is a daily process of dying to self and dedicating ourselves to serving our Master. Luke records the words of Jesus:

> Then he said to them all, "If anyone desires to come after Me, let him deny himself, and take up his cross daily, and follow Me. For whoever desires to save his life will lose it, but whoever loses his life for My sake will save it. For what profit is it to a man if he gains the whole world, and is himself destroyed or lost? For whoever is ashamed of Me and My words, of him the Son of Man will be ashamed when He comes in His own glory, and in His Father's, and of the holy angels."[198]

The high cost of discipleship demanded by Jesus caused many people to turn away from following Him. Jesus wasn't trying to attract large crowds; rather He wanted loyal disciples!

---

[196] John 15:8
[197] Galatians 5:19-23
[198] Luke 9:23-26

So pastor, church leader, how is your church doing in making disciples? Whatever the attendance may be on Sunday mornings, how many of those attendees would you be able to call 'disciples of Jesus Christ'?

No Other Way

Another reason that many churches today are trivializing their God-given mission is that many have lost their commitment to the exclusivity of the gospel. We see the gospel as a matter of taste, rather than exclusive truth.

Since Jehovah is the only true God that exists, logic concludes that there is no other true God. It is contradictory to claim that there is only one true God, Jehovah, and then claim that other gods are legitimate. The Christian church has affirmed its belief in the triune God ever since the Council of Constantinople in 297 A.D. The deity of Jesus Christ has remained a cardinal doctrine of the Christian church.

Arianism, named after its teacher, Arius (250-336 A. D.), says that Jesus was not truly God, but that he became God. This teaching was condemned as heresy, even though it still exists today in a cult group called Jehovah's Witnesses.

Our inclusive and politically correct society has adopted the axiom that there is no absolute truth. The vast majority of secular thinkers today believe that truth is relative and personal. "Your truth is your truth and my truth is my truth" according to the philosophers of our modern world. Therefore, the claim that Jesus Christ is the only way to heaven and to the Father is viewed as narrow-minded and bigoted.

The Bible in its entirety is the infallible word of God. Therefore, the recorded words of Jesus in John 14:6 must be accepted by all true Christians to be absolute truth. As Jesus spoke to the confused Thomas, he said "I am the way, the truth, and the life. No one comes to the Father except through Me."

The revived disciples, Peter and John, after the resurrection of Jesus Christ and the coming of the Holy Spirit at Pentecost, were under attack by the Jewish leaders. They had healed a lame man in the name of Jesus Christ and the general populace of Jerusalem were giving much attention to the message about Jesus Christ. The Jewish leaders sought to silence Peter and John in order to restore their own waning authority with the people. Bringing Peter and John out of prison, they questioned them as to their power and authority for healing the lame man. Peter, filled with the Holy Spirit, boldly replies:

> Rulers of the people and elders of Israel: if we this day are judged for a good deed done to a helpless man, by what means he has been made well, let it be known to you all, and to all the people of Israel, that by the name of Jesus Christ of Nazareth, whom you crucified, whom God raised from the dead, by Him this man stands here before you whole. This is the stone which was rejected by you builders, which has become the chief corner stone. Nor is there salvation in any other, for there is no

other name under heaven given among men by which we must be saved.[199]

Researcher George Barna shares some startling statistics regarding the beliefs of those who claim to be 'born-again' Christians.

One in four born-again Christians holds universalist-thoughts when it comes to salvation. Twenty-five percent of born-again Christians said all people are eventually saved or accepted by God. A similar proportion, 26 percent, said a person's religion does not matter because all faiths teach the same lessons. And an even higher proportion, 40 percent of born-again Christians said they believe Christians and Muslims worship the same God.[200]

A minority of American adults (40%) are persuaded that Jesus Christ lived a sinless life while He was on earth. Slightly less than two-thirds of the born again segment (62%) strongly believes that He was sinless. Similarly, only one-quarter of adults (28%) believe that it is impossible for someone to earn their way into Heaven through good behavior. Not quite half of all born again Christians (47%) strongly reject the notion of earning salvation through their deeds."[201]

---

[199] Acts 4:8-12

[200] http://www.freerepublic.com/focus/f-religion/2709756/posts

[201] https://www.barna.org/barna-update/21-transformation/252-barna-survey-examines-changes-in-worldview-among-christians-over-the-past-13-years#.VP4BCu90zCA

Barna defined universalism as the belief that all human beings will eventually be saved after death. The California-based research and polling firm defines born-again Christians as people who have made "a personal commitment to Jesus Christ that is still important in their life today, and who believe they will go to heaven after death because they confessed their sins and accepted Jesus Christ as their Savior."[202]

Because it is unpopular to believe that there is only one way to heaven, some pastors are even questioning this clear declaration by Jesus Himself. Jesus said,

> Enter by the narrow gate; for wide is the gate and broad is the way that leads to destruction, and there are many who go in by it. Because narrow is the gate and difficult is the way which leads to life, and there are few who find it.[203]

The human preference is to broaden the gate and broaden the way to heaven. It would be nice to believe that all people will eventually make it to heaven's glory but the Scriptures do not give us that option. All true believers in Jesus Christ must clearly assert that Jesus Christ is the one and only way to find eternal life with our heavenly Father. To say anything else is to deny that Jesus Christ spoke the truth.

Following the attacks upon the World Trade Center, September 11, 2001, the pressure increased upon Christian leaders to make accommodation for peace-loving Muslims. Dr. Joseph Stowell,

---

[202]   http://www.christianpost.com/news/many-born-again-christians-hold-universalist-view-barna-finds-49883/
[203] Matthew 7:13-14

fittingly, comments on the religious spin that followed that fateful tragic day.

The war on terror triggered a phenomenon that only added to the confusion about the authentic Jesus.

As Colin Nicholl has noted, soon after that horrible day in September, it became evident that it was politically necessary, for the sake of not alienating Arab nations we needed in the war against terror, to present Islam as a religion of peace and goodwill. Our president took great pains to make the point, both in public proclamations as well as in visits to several mosques. In a strange way, the September attack on America has become a PR coup for Islam. It is now mainstreamed alongside of Christianity and Judaism as a major player on the field of religion in America. This has enabled us to put another God into the mix of god's already on the god shelf of our emerging paganism. Islam, unlike Judaism, reveres Jesus; but like Judaism, it denies his unique claims, which only muddies the waters in terms of public perception.

In the midst of this effort to legitimize Islam, a church in Chicago area invited a Muslim to speak about his religion. The well-intentioned effort was staged to help followers of Christ understand that not all Muslims are hateful murderers and to engender an ongoing Christ-like love for Muslim people. In the course of the interview the Islamic devotee was speaking of the many similarities between Islam and Christianity. He said, "all of us - you believe in Jesus, I believe in Jesus. I believe in my Mohammed and all the

171

prophets. So our mission is to introduce people to God."

Not really.

Muslims believe that Jesus was a prophet of the highest order, but they do not believe that he is God, as he himself claimed to be. They deny that he was born of a virgin. They deny that he rose from the dead. And they reject the fact that his death was the final and ultimate atonement for sin.

There is no way that they believe in Jesus, like we do. Not the real Jesus. It was pure spin. But then "Jesus" gives Islam credibility - especially in America - so let's make Him fit.

But making Jesus fit is a problem. For him to fit, you have to twist and disfigure Jesus in serious ways. In order to become all things to all people, Jesus must be spun as not having said what the Bible affirms he said. A one-size-fits-all Jesus must be tolerant of everyone, judgmental toward none, kind, but not analytical, loving, but not disciplining, a moldable figment of every imagination, a bland, almost boring, toothless, inoffensive, non-divisive, disposable Jesus."[204]

Therefore, every church's pastors and lay leaders must take their stand. Will you clearly and unequivocally believe and teach that Jesus Christ is the only way to the Father? Unless you do, the Great Commission becomes unnecessary. If there are other ways to find eternal life in heaven, then

---

[204] Joseph M. Stowell, The Trouble With Jesus (Moody Publishers, Chicago, 2003) pages 79-80

there is no reasonable motivation to take the Great Commission seriously.

Local or World Missions

When a local church is considering its part in the fulfillment of the Great Commission, there is always a tension between the local mission of the church and our responsibility toward the rest of the world. In Acts 1:8 Jesus made it clear that every believer is to be involved, not only in their Jerusalem (local church), but also in their Judea (their state and country), and also in their Samaria (outcast groups for "the Jews had no dealings with the Samaritans")[205] and to the uttermost parts of the world (all other people-groups on this earth).

As Jesus addressed the disciples regarding His return and the end of the age, he said: "This gospel of the kingdom will be preached in all the world as a witness to all the nations, and then the end will come."[206] Jesus made a connection between His return and the completion of the church's task in fulfilling the Great Commission. The apostle Peter supports the idea that the return of Jesus Christ for His church can be 'hastened' by the faithful godly living of His followers.[207] Faithful godly living assumes that Christ's disciples are being faithful in preaching the gospel to all nations.

Many evangelical churches are taking this seriously by adopting 'unreached peoples groups' as an integral part of their mission outreach. Other evangelical churches, when their budgets are

---

[205] John 4:9
[206] Matthew 24:14
[207] 2 Peter 3:11-13

examined, are practically ignoring the fulfillment of the Great Commission. We find that ninety five percent or more of their dollars, are being spent on their local ministries. In many of our local evangelical churches there is almost no mention of missions beyond their local church; and there is minimal prayer emphasis for the worldwide mission of the church.

Local building programs are necessary, or so it seems, in our Western world cultures. The local church must have an adequate place to meet for worship and to carry out ministries that are effective in reaching our local populations. How do we define 'adequate'? We must seriously question the lavish expenditures upon unnecessary structures and accoutrements.

K. P. Yohannan reports in his book, Revolution in World Missions:

> I have spoken in churches that had millions of dollars invested in buildings - churches with pastors known as excellent Bible teachers with a heart of love for people. Yet, I have discovered that many of them have absolutely no missionary program of any kind.
>
> In preaching to one of these churches, I made the following statement: "While you claim to be evangelicals and pour time and life into learning more and more biblical truths, in all honesty, I do not think you believe the Bible.
>
> My listeners were shocked. But I continued.
>
> If you believed the Bible you say you believe, the very knowledge there is a real place called hell - where millions will go and spend

eternity if they die without Christ - would make you the most desperate people in the world to give up everything you have to keep missions and reaching the lost as your top priority.[208]

This tension is difficult to solve for pastors and local church leaders. What is the correct percentage that should go toward the mission beyond our borders? Each local church pastor and church leader must answer this question with sincere prayer and seeking the Holy Spirit's leadership.

A few churches have sought to tie world missions with local building programs. Raising funds for their local project, they have designated a percentage of the funds raised to strengthening their worldwide outreach.

Some Wise Strategies

Short-term missions projects, when well planned, are helpful in several ways. When people with the right skills and abilities are matched properly with the needed project on some world mission field, it can strengthen the work of the struggling church. Such a project can deepen the interest and prayer ministry of the local church, not only in the lives of the actual participants, but in the lives of those who remain at home. The interest and call of many committed world missionaries began through the actual experience of a short-term mission project.

New methods, such as training and supporting native pastors and evangelists versus sending

---

[208] K. P. Yohannan, Revolution in World Missions (gfa books, a division of Gospel for Asia, Carrollton, TX 75010, 36th printing, 2010) pages 131-132

American missionaries to other cultures, is proving to be much more cost efficient. To support a native missionary in India, for example, costs about forty to eighty dollars a month (United States currency), in contrast to supporting a missionary sent from the United States, which costs somewhere in the neighborhood of forty to sixty thousand dollars, or more, annually. In addition, the native missionary is already conversant in his native language and he is much more effective in communicating in his own culture.

K. P. Yohannan comments favorably concerning supporting national evangelists and pastors. He says:

> There is a vast difference between living at the same level as an Asian peasant - as national evangelists do - and living at even a modest Western standard . . . Our Western missionary, however, is faced with many additional costs. These include international air transportation, shipping of many possessions to the field, language schools, and special English-language schools for children and Western-style housing. National missionaries, on the other hand, live in villages on the same level as others in the community whom they are seeking to reach for Christ.

> The Western missionary also is faced with a visa and other legal fees, costs of communication with donors, extra medical care, import duties and requirements to pay taxes in his home country. The cost of food can be very high, especially if the missionary entertains other Westerners, employs servants to cook or eats imported foods.

Frequently host governments require foreign missionaries to meet special tax or reporting requirements, usually with payments required.

Clothing, such as shoes and imported Western garments, is costly. Many national missionaries choose to wear sandals and dress as the local people do.

For a Western missionary family with children, the pressure is intense to maintain a semblance of Western-style living. Frequently this is increased by the pressure and private schools where other students are the sons and daughters of international businessman and diplomats.

Finally, vacations and in-country travel or tourism are not considered essential by national missionaries as they are by most Westerners. The cost of imported English books, periodicals, records and tapes is also a big expense not part of the national missionary's lifestyle.

The result of all this is that Western missionaries often need 30 to 40 times more money for their support than does a national missionary.[209]

Western world churches may still need to send specialized missionaries to help teach in seminaries in foreign countries to assist in the task of equipping native pastors and evangelists. Many mission organizations have learned by their experiences that

---

[209] K. P. Yohannan, Revolution in World Missions (gfa books, a division of Gospel for Asia, Carrollton, TX 75010, 36th printing, 2010) pages 217-218

it is better to train native pastors and evangelists in their own country, rather than bringing them to seminaries in the Western world. When natives of Third World countries are brought to the United States or Canada for their training, they become so accustomed to living our lifestyle that they do not want to return to their native countries. Other specialized missionaries, such as Bible translation experts, are also needed to help with translating God's word into languages of unreached people groups.

Micro-loan programs are being established in many foreign countries as an effective tool in aiding native believers to be able to escape from poverty and to be able to support their families. Small loans, along with teaching management skills and accountability, make these ministries very effective.

The Western church model for missions has been one of 'the goers and the senders'. The 'goers' are the professional missionaries and the 'senders' are those faithful believers who pay the bills. The same model has become prevalent in the local church. Many evangelical Christians have come to view their pastors as the professionals who understand the Bible and who are paid to do the work of ministry.

This is not a plea to do away with the paid pastor. In a congregation of any size, there is a need for leadership and for biblical preaching that requires much time and effort. The New Testament teaches that we are to support those who teach the word to us.[210] The apostle Paul, however, took great pride in the fact that he supported his own ministry and mission. As Paul defends his apostleship in 1

---

[210] 1 Timothy 5:17-18; Luke 10:7

Corinthians 9, he asks and answers some very pertinent questions.

My defense to those who examined me, is this: do we have no right to eat and drink? Do we have no right to take along a believing wife, as do also the other apostles, the brothers of the Lord, and Cephas? Or is it only Barnabas and I who have no right to refrain from working? Whoever goes to war at his own expense? Who plants a vineyard and does not eat of its fruit? Or who tends the flock and does not drink of the milk the flock? Do I say these things as a mere man? Or does not the law say the same also? For it is written in the law of Moses, "You shall not muzzle an ox while it treads out the grain." Is it oxen God is concerned about? Or does He say it all together for our sakes? For our sakes, no doubt, this is written, that he who plows should plow in hope, and he who thrashes in hope should be partaker of his hope. If we have sown spiritual things for you, is it a great thing if we reap your material things? If others are partakers of this right over you, are we not even more? Nevertheless, we have not used this right, but endure all things lest we hinder the gospel of Christ." Do you not know that those who minister the holy things eat of the things of the temple, and those who serve at the altar partake of the offerings of the altar? Even so, the Lord has commanded that those who preach the gospel should live from the gospel. But I have used none of these things, nor have I written these things that it should be done so to me; for it would be better for me to die, than that anyone should make my boasting void. For if I preach the gospel, I have nothing to boast of, for necessity is laid upon me; yes, woe is me if I do not preach the gospel! For if I do this willingly, I have a reward; but if against my will, I have been entrusted with the stewardship. What is my reward then? That when I preach the gospel, I may present the gospel of Christ, without charge, that I may not abuse my authority in the gospel.[211]

The apostle Paul was a tent maker evangelist and missionary. The church at Antioch, through fasting and prayer, sensed that the Holy Spirit was appointing Paul and Silas to a special work of ministry. In Acts 13:3, we read: "Then, having fasted and prayed, and laid hands on them, they sent them away." Many evangelical believers are following a similar model. As trained professionals, and as businessmen, they are taking up residency in other countries. Through employment, they are paying their way and making a difference in the country they have chosen as their mission field. Not only are they serving their adopted country through their skills, but through their presence and their opportunities of friendship, they are sharing the gospel with the people of another nation.

The Need for Biblical Stewardship

K. P. Yohannan, quotes statistics from Barrett and Johnson, World Christian Trends: "The average North American Christian gives only fifty cents a week to global missions." This statistic is probably from the late 1990's; I suspect it is quite likely a lower amount in 2015. Yohannan goes on to say:

> Missions is the primary task of the church, our Lord's final command to us before his

---

[211] 1 Corinthians 9:4-18

ascension. Jesus died on the cross to start a missionary movement. He came to show God's love, and we are left here to continue that mission. Yet this most important task of the church is receiving less than one percent of all our finances.[212]

The financial crisis facing many evangelical churches and gospel ministries today is predicted to become even greater in the coming decade. John S. Dickerson writes about this in chapter four of his book, which he entitles, 'Bankrupt'. His dire predictions are based upon present happenings in American churches and ministries.

> Donations to many churches and ministries have plummeted 20 to 30 percent per year since the great recession pummeled the United States economy.

> We often tie the drop in giving to the drop in the economy. But a larger undercurrent is also at play. The generation that gives almost half of total donations began passing away about three years ago. (He is writing this in 2013.) Nearly one thousand of them are called home every day. Their funerals and memorials are quietly held every morning, afternoon, and evening in rural churches and metropolitan chapels across the country. Nobody seems to be noticing.

> Over the next twelve years, this faithful and reliable generation will pass away. As they do, total giving will decrease by as much as

---

[212] K. P. Yohannan, Revolution in World Missions (gfa books, a division of Gospel for Asia, Carrollton, TX 75010, 36th printing, 2010) page 152

half for typical evangelical ministries - nationally, regionally, and locally.[213]

Dickerson shares a little more gloom about the future.

> Simply put, the older contributors who fund evangelical ministries are passing off the scene. It is a fact that, on the whole, their kids and grandkids do not share their commitment to evangelical ministries (if their heirs are evangelical at all, as we will see in chapter five, Bleeding).

> Unless giving trends change significantly, evangelical giving across the board may drop by about seventy percent during the next twenty-five to thirty years. A recovery of the United States economy will not have bearing on dropping ministry income - unless generational patterns change drastically.[214]

If the great commission is ever to be fulfilled, we must do a much better job of teaching our children and our grandchildren what it means to be a disciple of Jesus Christ. We must teach the precepts of stewardship, not only verbally, but by example. A common characteristic of the millennial generation, those who profess to be Christians, is their lack of systematic giving of their financial means to the Lord and His church. They are motivated by emotional appeal rather than biblical principle.

Stewardship is the responsible and faithful use of what has been committed to you by another. Merriam Webster's dictionary defines stewardship as "the conducting, supervising, or managing of

---

213 John S. Dickerson, IBID, page 82
214 John S. Dickerson, IBID, page 84

something; especially, the careful and responsible management of something entrusted to one's care." Unfortunately, most people think of money when they think of biblical stewardship. Biblical stewardship is much more expansive in its scope. Our handling of material things will always reflect the depth of our devotion to our Lord Jesus. Biblical stewardship begins with the recognition that everything I am and everything I possess is given to me as a gift from God.

C. S. Lewis, in his book, Mere Christianity, says:

> Every faculty you have, your power of thinking or of moving your limbs from moment to moment, is given you by God. If you devoted every moment of your whole life exclusively to His service you could not give Him anything that was not in a sense his own already . . . It is like a small child going to its father and saying, 'Daddy, give me sixpence to buy you a birthday present.' It is all very nice and proper, but only an idiot would think that the father is sixpence to the good on the transaction.

To be a disciple of Jesus Christ means devoting ourselves totally to Him. It means that our hearts will be transformed so that our hearts will desire the will of God in our lives above anything else. When our hearts beat with God's heart, we will seek His power to be obedient to His Great Commission. Someone has said, "If you want to know your priorities in life, study your checkbook."

Pastors and church leaders, how are you doing in leading your churches? Does the annual budget of your church reflect God's priorities? How much time do you spend in prayer as you plan out your next year's ministry and budget? Do you do zero-based budgeting? Do you review each ministry and each budget line item to be sure that money is being well spent? Is the proportion of your budget that is set aside for missions, beyond your local church ministries, a proper percentage that reflects your churches involvement in fulfilling the Great Commission? Is Jesus Christ allowed to be the head of your local church in everything?

> A declining interest in missions is the sure sign that a church and people have left their first love. Nothing is more indicative of the moral decline of the West than Christians who have lost the passion of Christ for a lost and dying world. [215]

---

[215] K. P. Yohannan, Revolution in World Missions (gfa books, a division of Gospel for Asia, Carrollton, TX 75010, 36th printing, 2010) page 168

Chapter Nine

For Now or For Eternity

The 21st century western world man is a 'now' man. He is generally focused on the immediate, giving little thought to future, eternal realities. He has little interest in anything that does not profit him immediately in the here and now. He sees life as only lived once. Therefore he pursues the immediate practical benefit with gusto. The evangelical churches have often fallen into the trap of trivializing eternity while trying to connect with this misguided, dissatisfied, disillusioned man.

How? We see it in many of our churches in the content of our preaching and our teaching.

When you analyze much of the preaching of today's evangelical pastors you find pop psychology and self-improvement plans. You will hear practical ways to find a more comfortable and worry free life in the here and now through Jesus. Much of the preaching of today smacks more of the "health and wealth gospel" that coincides more with the American dream than it does with the teachings of Jesus Christ and His harassed and persecuted New Testament followers.

Pastor, before you preach your message on Sunday, ask yourself the question, "would I preach this way if I was preaching to the suffering saints in the Middle East, China, or some part of the persecuted world of believers?" Would this message ring true for them? If it does not apply to their lives, is it the truth of God for your congregation?

When preaching to the unsaved do we warn people of the impending judgment when all shall appear before God to give account? How long has it been since you heard a message warning humanity that they are rushing along toward an eternity in hell? How long has it been since you have heard a pastor say that we are all under the wrath of God for our sins? How long has it been since you have heard a pastor passionately appeal to people to repent and prepare to meet their God?

When God created man He created him with an eternal soul. While it was God's intention that man would walk in obedience to God and experience fellowship with God for eternity, man chose to disobey and rebel against God's authority. Man suffers the consequences of spiritual and physical death because of his sin.

Man's sin did not remove the eternal nature of his soul.
Every man will exist for eternity, whether it be in the presence of God or in the presence of Satan. Those who have been reconciled to God through repentance and faith in Jesus Christ will spend eternity in the presence of God in heaven's glory. Those who ignore Jesus Christ or reject the salvation provided by Christ on the cross will be separated from God forever in the place called the 'lake of fire' or hell.

What Is Eternity?

We human beings who live in the confinement of time have great difficulty in comprehending eternity. We think of the past as yesterday, or in the terms of years, decades, centuries, and even the millennia of past history. We seek to live today in a meaningful present. We dream of tomorrow and hope that our future days and years will improve over the past. But to comprehend eternity . . . the forever and ever and ever . . . is beyond our mental grasp. Theologian Millard J. Erickson helps us mull over the meaning and significance of eternity:

> Eternity is unlimited time and space. Isaiah 57:15: "For thus says the high and lofty One who inhabits eternity, whose name is Holy: 'I dwell in the high and holy place, and also with him who is of a contrite and humble spirit, to revive the spirit of the humble, and to revive the heart of the contrite.'" From eternity past God has always existed, without beginning. To eternity future God always will be, without ending.

> God has created man, and every man has a beginning. However, God has created man with an eternal soul, and he will exist for eternity future. No man will ever compete with God, nor will he ever become God. God is transcendent! By this we mean that God is separate from and independent of nature and humanity. God is not simply attached to, or involved in, his creation. He is also superior to it in several significant ways.[216]

Erickson continues:

> Even when redeemed and glorified, we will still be renewed human beings. We will never become God. He will always be God, and we will always be humans, so that there will always be a transcendence. Salvation consists

---

[216] Millard J. Erickson (Christian Theology, Volume 1, Baker book house, Grand Rapids, Michigan, 1983), page 312

in God's restoring us to what he intended us to be, not elevating us to what he is.

Reverence is appropriate in our relationship with God. Some worship, rightfully stressing the joy and confidence that the believer has in relationship to a loving heavenly Father, goes beyond that point to an excessive familiarity treating him as an equal, or worse yet, as a servant. If we have grasped the fact of the divine transcendence, however, this will not happen. While there are room and need for enthusiasm of expression, and perhaps even exuberance, which should never lead to a loss of respect. There will always be a sense of awe and wonder, of what Rudolf Otto called the mysterium tremendum. Although there are love and trust and openness between us and God, we are not equals. He is the Almighty, sovereign Lord. We are his servants and followers. This means that we will submit our wills to God; we will not try to make his will conform to ours. Our prayers will also be influenced accordingly. Rather than making demands in our prayers, we will pray as Jesus did, "not my will, but thine, be done."[217]

Eternality is an attribute of God. Eternity was not created by God, but is part of His nature. God is always "I AM!" God has always existed and never will go out of existence. God is always transcendent, separate from all that He has created. Man is always man and never will become God. Redeemed man is always redeemed man, privileged to be in God's presence and to serve, honor and glorify Him forever. God is not man's servant or slave, though God has chosen to show His grace and mercy in saving us from our sin. God has not

---

[217] Millard J. Erickson, IBID, page 318

provided His plan of salvation, by sending His Son as a sacrifice for our sin, out of obligation, but out of His grace and mercy.

Hell, What Is It?[218]

Frankly, this is a subject of which I would rather not write. There is a satanically induced aversion and resistance to the teaching about hell. Humanly, I prefer to write about peace and light and heaven. The thought of anyone having to spend even one second in hell is a thought that breaks my heart and ought to break every preacher's heart.

But this subject must be preached from the pulpits of our churches! If we are to be faithful to God, if we are to take seriously the teaching of the Bible, if we are to believe what Jesus Christ Himself taught, then we must preach clearly and forcefully about hell. We must compassionately and urgently warn all people of the impending doom that awaits anyone who dies without Christ as Savior. To fail in this is to fail to preach the truth of God's word! The word of God to Ezekiel is a warning to all of us as preachers of our responsibility to faithfully deliver God's message.

> Son of man, I have made you a watchman for the house of Israel; therefore hear a word from My mouth, and give them warning from Me: when I say to the wicked, 'You shall surely die,' and you give him no warning, or speak to warn the wicked from his wicked way, to save his life, that same wicked man

---

[218] This portion of this book is adapted from my previously self-published book, Norman P. Anderson, So You Want to Go to Heaven? God Tells You How! (Xulon Press, Fairfax, Virginia; 2002) chapter 7, pages 73-85, All rights owned by the author. Available on Amazon.

shall die in his iniquity; but his blood I will require at your hand. Yet, if you warn the wicked, and he does not turn from his wickedness, nor from his wicked way, he shall die in his iniquity; but you have delivered your soul.

Again, when a righteous man turns from his righteousness, and commits iniquity, and I lay a stumbling block before him, he shall die; because you did not give him warning he shall die in his sin, and his righteousness which he has done shall not be remembered; but his blood I will require at your hand. Nevertheless, if you warn the righteous man that the righteous should not sin, and he does not sin, he shall surely live because he took warning; also, you will have delivered your soul.[219]

Because of this natural repulsion we experience in thinking about hell, some theologians and liberal preachers are seeking to explain away the teaching of hell. Some have remade God to their own preference rather than accepting God as He has revealed Himself in the Bible. Some say that the God of the Old Testament is the God of punishment and wrath while the God of the New Testament is the God of love, mercy and grace. Not so! God has always been and always will be the holy and righteous God who punishes sin and reveals His wrath against sin. God has always been and always will be the God who loves sinners and has provided a way of escape from hell through His Son, Jesus Christ.

---

[219] Ezekiel 3:17-21

Many people fall into the trap of believing that which appeals to their preferences instead of accepting what the Scriptures reveal.

One very popular preference today is called universalism. Universalism is the view that whereas there is a hell, no one will ever occupy it. After all, Universalists say, there are many roads to heaven and everyone will eventually get there. All people will be saved because God is a God of love.

Another appealing preference is annihilationism. It teaches that people who do not accept Christ as their Savior may end up in hell but God will annihilate their souls at some point. So they will suffer for a time but it will not be everlasting in nature. They look at the fires of hell as being consuming fires which end the existence of sinners instead of punishing fires that are eternal in their punishing effects.

H. Richard Niebuhr firmly rebuked the liberal preachers and theologians who hold such views when he said that they believed in "a God without wrath [who] brought men without sin into a kingdom without judgment through the ministrations of a Christ without a cross."[220]

To leave out the teaching about hell is to sterilize the gospel to fit our human reasoning and our desires. Larry Dixon has stated it this way:

> The Gospel presented by many Christians today has no teeth. When the message about Jesus Christ is expressed only in terms of providing a superior joy or peace to that

---

[220] H. Richard Niebuhr, The Kingdom of God In America (Hamden,
Conn: Shoe String Press, 1956) page 193.

which the world offers, already joyful and peaceful pagans patronize the messenger and ignore the message . . . Christians need to faithfully proclaim the complete Gospel. That complete Gospel says, for example, that happiness without holiness is counterfeit Christianity, that self-fulfillment and a positive self-image do not bring eternal forgiveness. Such a complete Gospel proclaims that sins must either be pardoned or punished.[221]

Jonathan Edwards once said that the reason we find hell so offensive is because of our insensitivity to sin. If we realized the magnitude of our offensive rebellion against God, we would be convinced of God's righteousness in banishing all unforgiven sinners to hell.

The Reality of Hell

As sure as heaven is a real place, hell is a real place! Both places exist in God's created expanse. How do we know? Because the Bible tells us so.

The renowned Baptist preacher, Vance Havner, told of an experience he had as a pastor: When I pastored a country church, a farmer didn't like the sermons I preached on hell. He said, "Preach about the meek and lowly Jesus." I said, "That's where I got my information about hell.[222]

---

[221] Larry Dixon, The Other Side of the Good News (A Bridge Point Book, Victor Books, Wheaton, Illinois, 1992) page 22.

[222] George Sweeting, Who Said That? (Moody Press, Chicago, Illinois, 1994) page 231.

The reality of hell is taught plainly by Jesus Christ just as surely as He taught the reality of heaven. Surely He knows whereof He speaks. He is God, the Son, and Creator of all things, including hell itself. He would not have come to our world to suffer and die on the cross of Calvary in order to save us if there was no such reality as hell from which to save us. He would not have become "sin for us" (2 Corinthians 5:21) to save us from an eternal hell that doesn't really exist. Hear some of the words of Jesus about hell:

- Matthew 10:28: And do not fear those who kill the body but cannot kill the soul. But rather fear Him who is able to destroy both soul and body in hell.

- Mark 9:42-47: But whoever causes one of these little ones who believe in Me to stumble, it would be better for him if a millstone were hung around his neck, and he were thrown into the sea. If your hand causes you to sin, cut it off. It is better for you to enter into life maimed, rather than having two hands, to go to hell, into the fire that shall never be quenched— where 'their worm does not die and the fire is not quenched.' And if your foot causes you to sin, cut it off. It is better for you to enter life lame, rather than having two feet, to be cast into hell, into the fire that shall never be quenched - where 'their worm does not die and the fire is not quenched.' And if your eye causes you to sin, pluck it out. It is better for you to enter the kingdom of God with one eye, rather than having two eyes, to be cast into hell fire . . .

- In Luke 16:19-31, Jesus tells of the fate of the rich man who did not know God and had not found salvation in Jesus Christ. Verse 23 is clear about the reality of this place of suffering called hell. "And being in torments in Hades [hell], he lifted up his eyes and saw Abraham afar off, and Lazarus in his bosom." The expression "Abraham's bosom" is to be understood as being at the side of Abraham in the presence of God. John MacArthur notes in his study Bible: "Abraham's bosom. This same expression (found only here in Scripture) was used in the Talmud as a figure for heaven. The idea was that Lazarus was given a place of high honor, reclining next to Abraham at the heavenly banquet." [223]

The Necessity of Hell

The holiness of God necessitates hell. For God to be true to His own righteous and perfectly holy nature, he must remain free from any taint of that holiness. To tolerate sin of any kind would permanently contaminate God and make eternal righteousness impossible. We long for the coming day when we shall be welcomed to an existence in the presence of the holy God where all evil is forever banished and where its re-entrance is an impossibility. Then Jesus Christ will reign in righteousness forever.

Justice necessitates hell. Man's heart has always cried out for justice. A judgment day is coming in which the mills of justice will grind very, very fine and all will be made right! Those who have

[223] John MacArthur, The MacArthur Study Bible (Word Publishing, Nashville, London, Vancouver, Melbourne, 1997) page 1548

inflicted great evil upon the world and upon others will receive their just due. When we contemplate the awful evil works of devilish people such as Hitler, Stalin or Osama Bin Laden (you fill in the name of some other tyrant or despicable criminal), hell becomes a necessity. They must get their just due!

Are you ready for this? Sin itself necessitates hell. It is easy to see the justice of a Hitler or a serial killer being sent off to hell by God. Polls show that most people know someone personally or know of someone that they believe should be in hell. However, they do not believe that they themselves deserve to go to hell. This simply shows our insensitivity to the ugly nature of our sin. Any sin is a horrible, hideous reproach to the holiness of God. The Bible declares, "All have sinned and fall short of the glory of God . . ." Romans 3:23. It is for this reason that we all are declared to be "the children of wrath" (Ephesians 2:3) who rightly deserve to spend our eternity in hell. Praise God, He has given His Son to rescue us from such a fate.

We do not like to hear about this subject of hell. It is much more pleasant to avoid the subject. We prefer to hear our pastors speak on some more soothing topic. But preaching about hell is necessary in our modern world. Today you will hear more references to 'hell' on television and in movies than you will in the churches. When was the last time you can recall a pastor preaching a sermon on hell or warning about God's coming judgment? Even evangelical churches have tended to shy away from preaching and teaching this unpalatable subject because of a desire to appeal to worldly people with sensibility and polish. We do not want to turn off cultured people by "hell fire and brimstone" preaching.

Certainly pastors should not resort to speculative and dramatic preaching that goes beyond what the Bible teaches on the subject of hell. On the other hand, pastors must be faithful in warning of the judgment that is coming and hell that lies beyond the grave for unbelievers. Our silence rocks people to sleep, content to believe that they are in little danger. Larry Dixon puts it this way:

> A recent book on the Old Testament is entitled: Loving God and Disturbing Men: Preaching from the Prophets. That's what we Christians are to do: we are to love God and disturb people! Some believers need to hear the Gospel from the perspective of the love of God; others need to be told of the wrath of God. If the biblical doctrine of hell (in all its awesomeness as Jesus taught it) won't disturb the second group, nothing will.[224]

As someone once said, "the task of the preacher is to comfort the afflicted and to afflict the comfortable."

The Nature of Hell

In the Old Testament, the Hebrew word "sheol," translated as 'grave' at times and other times as 'hell' by the old King James Version of the Bible, refers to the place of the departed dead. It primarily refers to the place where the souls of unbelievers are held as they await the time of the final judgment. We will look at just a few references in the Old Testament.

---

[224] Larry Dixon, IBID, p. 186

- Deuteronomy 32:22 clearly speaks of a place where God's judgment fires will burn against the rebellious idolaters. "For a fire is kindled in My anger, and shall burn to the lowest hell (Sheol); it shall consume the earth with her increase, and set on fire the foundations of the mountains."

- Psalm 9:17: "The wicked shall be turned into hell (Sheol), and all the nations that forget God."

- The psalmist seeks for God's judgment upon his enemies, those who had claimed to be his friends. Psalm 55:15 says: "Let death seize them; Let them go down alive into hell (Sheol), for wickedness is in their dwellings and among them."

- The Psalmist expresses his gratitude to God for delivering his soul from "sheol" in Psalm 86:13: "For great is Your mercy toward me, and You have delivered my soul from the depths of Sheol."

The New Testament reveals much more about this eternal place called hell. One of the Greek words used to describe hell is the word 'Gehenna.' It appears in Matthew 5:22:

> But I say to you that whoever is angry with his brother without a cause shall be in danger of the judgment. And whoever says to his brother, 'Raca!' shall be in danger of the council. But whoever says, 'You fool!' shall be in danger of hell (Gehenna) fire.

Gehenna originally referred to the Valley of Hinnom outside of Jerusalem. In this valley was the garbage dump where the fires burned incessantly. For the Jews Gehenna became the synonym for the place of torment in the future life. Hell can be considered the cosmic garbage dump made by God for the purpose of disposing of all that is evil and would contaminate his eternal kingdom.

The Greek word, 'Hades', translated as 'hell' by the original King James Version of the New Testament, refers to the place where the souls of unbelievers are held until the final resurrection, when they will appear before God for final sentencing. They will then be cast into the final eternal hell which is called the lake of fire or the lake of burning brimstone. We read of the final judgment called the Great White Throne judgment in Revelation 20:11-15.

> Then I saw a great white throne and Him who sat on it, from whose face the earth and the heaven fled away. And there was found no place for them. And I saw the dead, small and great, standing before God, and books were opened. And another book was opened, which is the Book of Life. And the dead were judged according to their works, by the things which were written in the books. The sea gave up the dead who were in it, and Death and Hades delivered up the dead who were in them. And they were judged, each one according to his works. Then Death and Hades were cast into the lake of fire. This is the second death. And anyone not found written in the Book of Life was cast into the lake of fire.

Here are some of the facts that the Bible discloses about this place called hell.

- Hell is a place where there is eternal punishment. There will be suffering forever. Jesus speaks of a place where "their worm dies not and the fire is not quenched." (Mark 9:44, 46 and 48.) Note also Jesus' words as He teaches about the judgment of the nations at His second coming. Matthew 25:46. "And these will go away into everlasting punishment, but the righteous into eternal life."

- Hell is a place of fire and burning. Is there literal fire or is this just symbolic? My interpretation is that there is literal fire, although the fire there does not consume but rather torments forever. If it is symbolic of torment, it nevertheless speaks of a horrible place where such burning torment does not end. Even in Hades, the rich man that Jesus refers to in Luke 16, speaks of "being tormented in this flame." (Verse 24).

C. S. Lewis states: The prevalent image of fire is significant because it combines the ideas of torment and destruction. Now it is quite certain that all these expressions are intended to suggest something unspeakably horrible, and any interpretation which does not face that fact is, I am afraid, out of court from the beginning.[225]

- Hell is a place prepared for the devil and his evil angels. Matthew 25:41 says: Then He will also say to those on the left hand, 'depart from Me you cursed, into the everlasting fire prepared for the devil and his angels.

God does not desire that any human being should end up in hell.

---

[225] C. S. Lewis, The Problem of Pain (New York: Macmillan Publishers, 1962) page 125

2 Peter 3:9 says: "The Lord is not slack concerning His promise, as some count slackness, but is longsuffering toward us, not willing that any should perish but that all should come to repentance." However, those who resist Christ's appeal of love and His provision of pardon for sin through the cross, will be banished to this final eternal dwelling place prepared for Satan and his rebellious angels.

- Hell is a place where the sinner will continue in his sin forever. When the judgment of God is poured out in the end times, even then men will not repent. Rather they will persist in their anger against God and they will blame God for their suffering. Revelation 16:9 says: "And men were scorched with great heat, and they blasphemed the name of God who has power over these plagues; and they did not repent and give Him glory." This is the way it will also be in hell. The inhabitants of hell will be firmly set in their rebellion against God forever.

- Hell is a place of banishment from God forever. 2 Thessalonians 1:6-10 describes this final fate for unbelievers.

> Since it is a righteous thing with God to repay with tribulation those who trouble you, and to give you who are troubled rest with us when the Lord Jesus is revealed from heaven with His mighty angels in flaming fire taking vengeance on those who do not know God, and on those who do not obey the gospel of our Lord Jesus Christ. These shall be punished with everlasting destruction from the presence of the Lord and from the glory of His power, when He comes, in that Day, to be glorified in His saints and to be admired

among all those who believe, because our testimony among you was believed.

Some people have said to me, "Well, if I go to hell, at least all my friends will be there." This will be of little comfort when you wake up to the fact that there is no companionship in hell. Abandoned to Satan and his cohorts, you are surrounded and invaded completely with evil. You are shut out from all that is good and all that has to do with God. What a horrible destiny!

Eternity is very important for unbelievers. We are all sinners, but only those who come to realize their desperate condition and turn to Jesus Christ, the Savior, will escape hell's punishment. Unfortunately, too many sinners never come to the realization that they are lost and under the wrath of God. The Scriptures say,
"it is appointed for men once to die, and after this the judgment."[226] Therefore let us not fail to continually warn people of their peril. Preach the gospel and point people to the only refuge, Jesus Christ.

The Believer and Eternity

Eternity is also very important for believers. All born-again believers are on their way to heaven and will spend eternity with God. They are secure in knowing that their sins are all washed away and they will never perish. They are safely held in the hands of God and no one will ever be able to snatch them out of His hands.[227] Nothing will ever be able

---

[226] Hebrews 9:27
[227] John 10:27-30

to separate believers from the love of God in Christ Jesus.[228]

Eternity is important for believers, not just because they will dwell with Jesus Christ and God the Father forever, but eternity should impact how believers live their lives here and now.

The preaching and teaching in your church ought to equip believers to live in such a manner that will bring honor and glory to God. In many of our evangelical churches our preaching and teaching is encouraging cultural Christianity rather than biblical Christian discipleship.

We often hear it said, "You are so heavenly minded that you are no earthly good!" C. S. Lewis would respond to such a comment, "It is only as you are heavenly minded that you are any earthly good."

The eternal destiny and reward of the believer in heaven is the ultimate motivation for the Christian to follow his Master's challenge.

> "If anyone desires to come after me, let him deny himself, and take up his cross daily and follow me. For whoever desires to save his life will lose it, but whoever loses his life for my sake will save it. For what profit is it to a man if he gains the whole world, and is himself destroyed or lost?"[229]

Jesus taught the Pharisees, as they were seeking to find fault with Him, that He is the Good Shepherd and that He is also the door to the sheep fold.[230] In John 10:10, He says, "The thief does not come

---

228 Romans 8:38-39
229 Luke 9:23-25
230 John 10:1-18

except to steal, and to kill, and to destroy. I have come that they may have life, and that they may have it more abundantly." What is the abundant life? Much of our evangelical preaching and teaching today seeks to assure that Jesus will make you plentifully rich, abundantly healthy and continually comfortable. What a travesty to interpret Jesus words in this way.

What Jesus actually taught is far removed from this wrong interpretation of the abundant life. Jesus taught that in this world we would have tribulation and testing.[231] He also taught His disciples that His followers should expect to be persecuted and even put to death. The servant is not above his master; and if they treated God, the Son, in such hideous ways, His followers should expect the same kind of treatment.[232]

The abundant life that Jesus promises us is not health and wealth. It is not a life free of trouble. Rather, His promise is that we would be hated and persecuted by the world because the world does not know the Father.

What then is the abundant life? It is an intimate relationship and fellowship with Jesus Christ and with our heavenly Father. It is indescribable peace that He promises in the midst of suffering and persecution and rejection. It is the joy of our salvation, knowing that in this world we will suffer with Him, but in His kingdom we will reign with Him. It is the promise of our Savior, that we will never be separated from His love. It is the promise of our Great Shepherd, that He will care for us, that He will lead us in green pastures, and by still waters. The promise given by Christ through the

---

[231] John 16:33
[232] John 15:18-21

writer of Hebrews, as he wrote to the suffering Hebrew Christians, is a promise to us as well. "I will never leave you nor forsake you." So we may boldly say: "The Lord is my helper; I will not fear. What can man do to me?"[233]

Eternal Rewards for Believers

The Bible teaches that all believers will stand before the judgment seat of Christ. We will give account of how we as believers have lived our lives. As the apostle Paul was teaching the Corinthian church about the believer's new body, which he will receive in glory, he reminded them of the judgment of believers. He reminded them that because we will appear before Jesus Christ to give account, we therefore should always make it our aim to be well pleasing to Him.[234] The apostle Paul had written in his first letter to the Corinthian church about the judgment that would come upon believer's works. It would be a judgment of fire that would test the eternal nature of the believer's works.[235] Those whose works endure through the testing fire will receive their rewards. Those whose works are consumed by the fire do not get rewards; instead, they suffer loss.

The Bible also teaches that God will reward us for faithful service to Him. Many professing believers say that they don't really care about rewards in heaven, as long as they get there. However, it will be a sad day for many believers when they fail the test of enduring works, and they fail to hear the Lord's "Well done, good and faithful servant."[236]

---

[233] Hebrews 13:5b – 6
[234] 2 Corinthians 5:9-10
[235] 1 Corinthians 3:10-15
[236] Matthew 25:21,23

The New Testament teaches about several crowns that are promised to faithful and fruitful believers. The apostle Paul teaches that there are five different crowns that believers can earn:[237]

• The Soul Winners Crown (Philippians 4:1; 1 Thessalonians 2:19) for leading people to Christ.

• The Incorruptible Crown of Self Denial (1 Corinthians 9:25) for sacrificing and training hard in order to follow Christ at any price.

• The Crown of Righteousness (2 Timothy 4:8) for longing for the appearing of Christ at His second coming. Living in the light of the imminent return of Christ will dramatically affect our every thought and action!

• The Crown of Life (The Martyr's Crown) (James 1:12; Revelation 2:10) for suffering persecution even to the point of death for the sake of Christ.

• The Crown of Glory (The Pastor's Crown) for shepherding well the flock of God (1 Peter 5:4).

All the crowns will one day be laid at the feet of Jesus. (Revelation 4:10-11) All glory and honor and praise and riches and wisdom belong to Jesus Christ.

So eternity matters! Pastors, church leaders, I appeal to you not to neglect the preaching and teaching of eternal values. Do not fall into the trap of neglecting eternity while focusing so strongly on the present. May every gospel preaching church and every faithful pastor heed the words of the apostle Paul to Titus.

---

[237] Gleaned this summary from a blog; Dr. Roger Barrier, What Really Matters in Life? June 24, 2015

For the grace of God that brings salvation has appeared to all men, teaching us that, denying ungodliness and worldly lusts, we should live soberly, righteously, and godly in the present age, looking for the blessed hope and glorious appearing of our great God and Savior Jesus Christ, who gave Himself for us, that He might redeem us from every lawless deed and purify for Himself His own special people, zealous for good works. Speak these things, exhort, and rebuke with all authority. Let no one despise you."[238]

---

[238] Titus 2:11-15

Chapter Ten

A Strong Moral Stand in a Rotting World

One of the greatest challenges facing the church in America today is the challenge of the trivializing and marginalizing of God and Christians in the public square. It has become widely accepted that the only group of people in the United States of America who can be attacked with impunity are evangelical Christians.

As the Christian church is trivialized by a more militant secular culture, many churches and many Christians are failing to stand for God and truth? Many believers are choosing the silent safe route in order to maintain peace. Is your church equipping your people to lovingly stand for truth, for God and biblical morality, as our culture becomes less friendly toward believers?

Morality is simply a system of belief as to what is right and what is wrong. Strictly speaking, every person has a system of morality. Every religion, even atheistic religion, has a system of morality.

C. S. Lewis, in his book, Mere Christianity, argues that every culture of the world possesses certain moral guidelines. God has placed within each human being a sense of right and wrong. Every person's conscience either approves or disapproves of his behaviors.

The founders of the United States of America based this nation upon biblical morality. Throughout the history of this nation, Judeo-Christian morality has been generally accepted in the public square. President John Adams said:

> We have no government armed with power capable of contending with human passions unbridled by morality and religion. Avarice, ambition, revenge, or gallantry, would break the strongest cords of our Constitution as a whale goes through a net. Our Constitution was made only for a moral and religious people. It is wholly inadequate to the government of any other.[239]

The infamous Madelyn Murray O'Hare is often credited with the removal of Scripture reading and prayer from the public schools of the United States. While she fought against this practice in the city of Baltimore, Maryland, it was through court cases filed by others in 1962 and 1963, that state-sponsored prayers were removed from the public schools. This led to much debate about the conflict of the 'establishment' clause and the 'free-exercise' clause in the First Amendment. While the courts clearly did not forbid a student's right to pray, as long as the student's praying did not interfere with the work of others, these rulings were the beginning of the removal of God from the public square.

There is definitely a growing segment of our population that favors "freedom from religion" in place of "freedom of religion". The Freedom From Religion Foundation (FFRF) exists for the purpose of removing religion, especially Christianity, from our society. The co-president is Dan Barker, a former minister and Christian song writer for nineteen years before "losing his faith in his faith"

---

[239] Message from John Adams to the Officers of the First Brigade of the Third Division of the Militia of Massachusetts John Adams, Letter written October 11, 1798

in the early 1980's. The other co-president is his wife, Annie Laurie Gaylor, who founded the organization with her mother in 1978.

Barker says he used to enjoy leading people in the sinner's prayer. He is now an avowed and hostile atheist who spends his time traveling the nation, publicly debating the legitimacy of the Bible and the validity of Jesus as an actual historical figure. FFRF spends its time and money in filing lawsuits seeking the removal of any vestige of Christianity. They seek to intimidate governments to remove "In God We Trust" insignia and decals from police cars and other public service organizations.[240]

In the last fifty years, a decline in the acceptance of Judeo-Christian morality in our country continues to progress. Secularism expands its influence and postmodern thought patterns are impacting even those who call themselves 'Christian'. Secular worldviews and other religious worldviews are colliding with the Judeo-Christian worldview. Morality is no longer about truth versus error, or good versus evil. The prophet Isaiah describes our modern culture even as he described the culture of his day in Israel. "Woe to those who call evil good, and good evil; who put darkness for light, and light for darkness; who put bitter for sweet, and sweet for bitter!"[241]

Deconstructionism and Authority

What is deconstructionism? It is a philosophy of thought developed in 1967 by French philosopher

---

[240] Article in Decision Magazine, BGEA; November, 2015 edition, Standing Up To Radical Atheists, Charles Chandler, pages 4-7
[241] Isaiah 5:20

Jacques Derrida.[242] He was greatly influenced by Frederick Nietzsche. Nietzsche's point in 'Daybreak' is that, standing at the end of modern history, modern thinkers know too much to be deceived by the illusion of reason. Reason, logic, philosophy and science are no longer solely sufficient as the royal roads to truth.[243]

Derrida himself claimed that all of his essays were attempts to define what deconstruction is. Deconstruction is necessarily complicated and difficult to explain, since it actively criticizes the very language needed to explain it.[244] Basically, Derrida questioned all authority and the ability to know anything with certainty. The influence of Derrida and his followers has led us to the point in our culture where absolute truth is believed to be unknowable, if indeed it ever existed. It has led our modern culture to believe that 'your truth' and 'my truth' are both plausible and acceptable truths, even though they may be totally contradictory.

Totally contradictory statements cannot both be true. The Bible states clearly that Jesus Christ is

---

[242] Derrida first used the term "Deconstruction" in his work "Of Grammatology", French version, p. 25 (Les Éditions de Minuit, 1967, ISBN 978-2-7073-0012-6). On this page Derrida states that the occidental history of sign is essentially theological with reference to Logocentrism. Derrida starts a metaphysical approach of semiology. He states that the concept of sign and deconstruction work are always exposed to misunderstanding. He uses the term "méconnaissance" probably in reference to Jacques Lacan who rejected the belief that reality can be captured in language. On the same page Derrida states that he will try to demonstrate that there is no linguistic sign without writing.

[243] https://en.wikipedia.orgwikideconstruction#Deconstructing_History

[244] Derrida, 1985, p. 4

God the Son, and that He is the only way to God, the heavenly Father.[245] Islam teaches that Jesus is only one of the prophets and that he is lesser than Mohammed. Islam does not acknowledge that Jesus is God, much less the only way to eternal life. These contrasting beliefs are polar opposites; and they both cannot be true. Both of them could be untrue. If the first statement is true, then the second one must be false. If the second statement is true, then the first one must be false.

Douglas Groothuis says that French philosopher, Jacques Derrida, deconstructed texts to deny them any authority and these methods have been used on the Bible. Therefore deconstructionism destroys the possibility of any foundation for truth. Deconstructionism replaces the authority of God and His revealed word in the Bible with individual man's opinion. Every individual human being decides what any text means, whether it be the Bible, the Constitution of the United States or any other document.

The Redefinition of Marriage

The leaders of the sexual revolution in America are following a four-part strategy: seek to normalize aberrant sexual behavior, legalize it, celebrate it, and then ostracize anyone who doesn't endorse it.

News came on June 26, 2015 that the Supreme Court ruled in favor of same-sex marriage. In a five to four ruling the Supreme Court ruled that the Constitution requires all fifty States to provide for same-sex marriage. Justice Kennedy was the deciding vote and he wrote the majority opinion. This is the most recent example of the

---

[245] John 8-10; 14:6; etc.

deconstruction of the Constitution by the liberal wing of the Supreme Court as they seek to justify their advocacy of cultural change. The words written by the authors of the Constitution have no meaning, and no significance, if every reader of the Constitution decides for himself what it means.

The Constitution says nothing about marriage because this was an issue to be left to the governance of the separate States. The liberal wing Supreme Court defended their ruling with the fourteenth Amendment's requirement for "equal protection of the law."

Section one of the fourteenth Amendment states:

> All persons born or naturalized in the United States, and subject to the jurisdiction thereof, are citizens of the United States and of the state wherein they reside. No state shall make or enforce any law which shall abridge the privileges or immunities of citizens of the United States; nor shall any state deprive any person of life, liberty, or property, without due process of law; nor deny to any person within its jurisdiction the equal protection of the laws.

The Supreme Court, by a narrow five to four margin, stripped all Americans of our freedom to debate and decide marriage policy through the democratic process. Instead of interpreting and applying the law, which is its proper role in our system of government, the Court invented a new constitutional right. It legislated a new law, rather than interpreting current law.

Legislating is the work of Congress. Interpreting the law is the work of the Supreme Court. So by one unconstitutional act, the Supreme Court replaced the definition of marriage between one man and one woman which has stood since the creation of man. In so doing, the Supreme Court has usurped the role of God. As Mike Huckabee stated in a recent presidential debate, "The Supreme Court is not the Supreme Being!"

Dr. John Hoeldtke, of Flame Ministries, comments:

> "The Supreme Court is not a sacrosanct entity. It is made up of very fallible human beings. In its history there have been many poor and bad decisions. To think of just a few we could consider Dred Scott v. Sanford (1856), Korematsu v. United States (1944), and Roe v. Wade (1973).[246]

Chief Justice Roberts wrote: "Just who do we think we are?" . . . "The Majority's decision is an act of the will, not legal judgment. The right it announces has no basis in the Constitution or this Court's precedents." Justice Scalia, in his dissent wrote: "A system of government that makes the People subordinate to a committee of nine unelected lawyers does not deserve to be called a democracy . . . Thus, when the rights of persons are violated, the Constitution requires redress by the courts." Justice Thomas added: "to allow the policy question of same-sex marriage to be considered and resolved by a select, patrician, highly unrepresentative panel of nine is to violate a principle even more fundamental than no taxation without representation: no social transformation without representation." Justice Alito also weighed in: "I assume that those who cling to old beliefs will be able to whisper their thoughts in the recesses of their homes, but if they

---

[246] Dr. John Hoeldtke, Flame Ministries Newsletter, May, 2015, Box 3333, Everett, WA, 98213

repeat those views in public, they will risk being labeled as bigots and treated as such by governments, employers, and schools."

We have yet to see what this decision of the Supreme Court will mean in the free exercise of religion in our nation. Dr. Franklin Graham recently wrote:

> For some time now, I've been warning about the coming storm of religious persecution and oppression in America.
> Over the course of the past year, I've become increasingly convinced that the storm is no longer just approaching, it is hard upon us.
>
> The threats to the historic and sacred history of our nation's religious liberty are advancing on several prominent fronts.[247]

Graham quotes a young Canadian adult, Dawn Stefanowicz, one of six adult children of gay parents, who filed an amicus brief with the US Supreme Court, asking for the court to maintain the traditional definition of marriage. In an article written for 'Public Discourse', an online publication of the Witherspoon Institute, she wrote:

> I want to warn America to expect severe erosion of First Amendment freedoms if the U.S. Supreme Court mandates same-sex marriage. The consequences have played out in Canada for 10 years now, and they are truly Orwellian in nature and scope.

---

[247] Franklin Graham, Article: 'America, The Storm Is upon Us' (Decision Magazine, July-August, 2015, published by Billy Graham Evangelistic Association, Charlotte, North Carolina), page 6

In Canada, freedoms of speech, press, religion, and association have suffered greatly due to government pressure. The debate over same-sex marriage taking place in the United States could not legally exist in Canada today. Because of legal restrictions on speech, if you say or write anything considered hateful (including, by definition, anything questioning same-sex marriage), you could face discipline, termination of employment or prosecution by the government.[248]

Franklin Graham states further:

Marriage represents the very foundation of human social order. Everything of value sits on that base. Institutions, governments, prosperity, religious liberty, and the welfare of children are all dependent on its stability. When it is weakened or undermined, the entire superstructure begins to wobble.[249]

Pastor, church leader, Bible teacher, are you preparing God's redeemed people to stand firm for God and His revealed word when the day of persecution comes?

What Is Marriage?

Ever since the creation of man, marriage has always been a union of one man and one woman. Down through the centuries, in almost every culture, marriage has been defined as the union of one man and one woman. The U. S. Supreme Court, in its recent ruling, has chosen arbitrarily to redefine the institution of marriage in our nation. Does the

---

[248] Franklin Graham, IBID, page 7
[249] Franklin Graham, IBID, page 6

unconstitutional act of five liberal judges change what marriage is? Just because they decide to call the union between two men or two women 'marriage' does not make it marriage. Such a union can never be consummated and will never be marriage, no matter how many courts declare it to be such. This is just as absurd and nonsensical as to call a fish a bird, or to call a dog a cat. Changing its name does not change its nature one iota.

Here is a little historical perspective.[250]

> In his first American dictionary, Noah Webster defined marriage as "the legal union of a man and woman for life," which served the purposes of "preventing the promiscuous intercourse of the sexes . . . promoting domestic felicity, and . . . securing the maintenance and education of children."[251] An influential 19th-century treatise defined marriage as "a civil status, existing in one man and one woman legally united for life for those civil and social purposes which are based in the distinction of sex."[252] The first edition of Black's Law Dictionary defined marriage as "the civil status of one man and one woman united in law for life."[253]

The dictionary maintained essentially that same definition for the next century.

Glenn Stanton comments on his blog:

---

[250] https://supreme.justia.com/cases/federal/us/57
[251] An American Dictionary of the English Language (1828)
[252] J. Bishop, Commentaries on the Law of Marriage and Divorce 25 (1852)
[253] Black's Law Dictionary 756 (1891)

The highest court in our land decided - ultimately by the vote of one man, Justice Kennedy - that our great Constitution gives a man the right to marry another man, and a woman the right to marry another woman. This was not about so-called "marriage equality", but a dramatic marriage redefinition, changing this essential institution into a genderless institution where husband and wife do not require one another, where children do not need their mother and father, and where there is nothing uniquely important about male or female for the family. They become merely preferential or sentimental.[254]

Marriage is God ordained as a relationship between a man and a woman, and God has established marriage for as long as mankind exists. Genesis 1:26-28 clearly states:

Then God said, 'Let Us make man in Our image, according to Our likeness; let them have dominion over the fish of the sea, over the birds of the air, and over the cattle, over all the earth and over every creeping thing that creeps on the earth.' So God created man in His own image; in the image of God He created them; male and female He created them. Then God blessed them, and God said to them, 'Be fruitful and multiply; fill the earth and subdue it'.

In Genesis 2:24, we read: Therefore a man shall leave his father and his mother and be joined to his wife, and they shall become one flesh.

[254] The True Story of Marriage, by Glenn T. Stanton, (http://moody.actonsoftware.com/cdnr/53/acton/attachment/8780/f-01ec/1/-/-/-/-/header.png)

God's authoritative word declares for all time what marriage is, and no man's decision will ever change that definition.

While Jesus was being confronted by the Pharisees, in their attempt to find something against Jesus, they asked Him, "Is it lawful for a man to divorce his wife for just any reason?" As Jesus responded to them, He clearly affirmed marriage as a bond between a man and a woman.

> Have you not read that He who made them at the beginning made them male and female, and said, 'for this reason a man shall leave his father and mother and be joined to his wife, and the two shall become one flesh'? So then, they are no longer two but one flesh. Therefore what God has joined together let not man separate.[255]

In Ephesians 5:22-33, the apostle Paul uses the marriage of a husband (man) and a wife (woman) as an illustration of the relationship of Christ and His church. When Paul is laying down qualifications for pastors and for deacons, he clearly states that they must be "the husband of one wife."[256] It is very clear from the Scriptures that marriage is defined in only one way; it is the union of one man and one woman.

Is Homosexuality Sin?

God alone determines what is right or wrong. He is holy and righteous in every aspect of His Being. Through His divine revelation in the Bible, God has

---

[255] Matthew 19:3-6
[256] 1 Timothy 3:2, 12; Titus 1:6

made known to us His will for our lives. He has also revealed to us that which is sinful, wicked and an abomination in His sight.

We do not look to our culture to define what is right or wrong, nor do we look to the Supreme Court of the United States to determine what is right or wrong. Just because the finite judges of the Supreme Court rule that something is right does not make it right in God's sight. Just because sin becomes more popular and widely accepted by our culture, it is no less sinful in God's sight. Augustine is attributed to have said, "Wrong is wrong, even if everybody is doing it, and right is right, even if nobody is doing it."

God is the creator of all things. So the primary question is "What was God's original plan for the human race?" When God created man, He called him, Adam. Adam was the epitome of God's creation and no mate was found appropriate for Adam. So God made Eve out of one of Adam's ribs and gave her to Adam as an appropriate helpmate for him. God bonded them together in the first marriage ceremony and commanded them that they should care for the earth, and that they should procreate so that the earth would be populated with human beings.[257]

Natural law informs us of the impossibility of two men or two women being able to procreate. If all human beings cohabited with their same-sex, the human race would cease to exist in one generation. Therefore, we must conclude, according to natural law, that homosexuality is not appropriate and is opposed to God's design for humanity.

---

[257] Genesis 2: 20-35

Dr. Armand M. Nicholi, a faculty member of Harvard Medical School's Department of psychiatry, says:

> No society, past or present, has ever tolerated the institutionalization of homosexuality, for to do so would be to sow the seeds for its own extinction because homosexuality undermines the basic unit of society - the family - and of course precludes procreation, which means extinction of the human race. [258]

According to the Bible, every perversion of human sexuality outside of marriage is sinful. Fornication and adultery are violations of God's intended holy marriage of a man and a woman who commit themselves to each other as long as God spares them from death. Fornication refers to sexual relationships between an unmarried man and an unmarried woman. Adultery refers to the violation of the marriage commitment by sexual relationships outside of marriage. Fornication and adultery are sinful sexual behaviors between people of the opposite sexes. Homosexuality is viewed in Scripture as sexual behavior between two people of the same sex. Because it is against the laws of nature, homosexuality takes on another level of sinfulness. John Jefferson Davis makes this comment:

> Man, as a consequence of disobedience, is marked by the curse (Genesis 3:16-19). His labor and his sexual life reflect the disordering and rupturing of the divine human relationship. The marriage relationship between image bearers, intended to be a

---

[258] Armand R. Nicholi, (cited in the Presbyterian Layman, June/July, 1978) page 6

reflection of God's love for man, is instead marked by lust, violence, and the struggle for dominance and power. Homosexuality is simply one expression among many of the basic disordering of human life; all lust, whether heterosexual or homosexual, violates the divine law and reflects man's fallen nature. The Bible looks not to the social environment for the source of the human dilemma, but to the heart of man himself.[259]

Lest I be branded a homophobe, let me make it crystal clear that all human beings are sinful beings. We are all children of God's wrath because of our sin. We are all in need of cleansing and forgiveness by God through the shed blood of Christ on the cross. Outside of His redemption and transformation of our hearts, we all are deserving of separation from God in hell. Thankfully all of us can repent and turn to Jesus Christ, trusting in Him to save us from our sins and from hell itself. God grants forgiveness and eternal life with Him to all repentant believers who trust Jesus Christ as Redeemer and Savior.

There are many today who seek to justify homosexuality as simply an alternate lifestyle. They seek to explain away the message of the Bible that clearly teaches homosexuality as a behavior that is judged as sinful by God. Michael Ukleja said: "Only towering cynicism can pretend that there is any doubt about what the Scriptures say about homosexuality."[260] A person must do a lot of deconstructing of the Scriptures in order to arrive at

---

[259] John Jefferson Davis (Evangelical Ethics: Issues Facing the Church Today, Presbyterian and Reformed Publishing Company, Phillipsburg, New Jersey, 1985), pages 114-115
[260] P. Michael Ukleja, (Homosexuality in the Old Testament, Bibliotheca Sacra 140, 1983), pages 259-266

a justification of homosexuality in God's sight. Therefore, let us examine the clear teachings of the Bible regarding homosexuality.

The first reference to homosexuality in the Bible is found in Genesis 19:1-11, where Abraham's nephew, Lot, is entertaining the two angels sent to Sodom to investigate the outcry against the sins of the cities of Sodom and Gomorrah. Lot has received the two angels into his home as his guests. In the evening, the men of Sodom, come banging on his door, demanding that Lot bring the two angels (who appear as men), so that they may 'know' them. The New International Version properly and plainly translates the Hebrew word 'yada', "that we can have sex with them."

D. S. Bailey demonstrates the extent to which advocates for the homosexual cause will go, when he says that the men of Sodom were simply desiring to get better acquainted with these visitors and display hospitality to them.[261] Bailey's interpretation has become the standard argument in the pro-homosexual circles. This is an impossible interpretation that violates the context completely. Whatever you think of Lot's proposal to them to offer his two virgin daughters to them that they may violate them sexually, it is abundantly clear that the intention of the men of Sodom was to have homosexual relations with these two male guests. Jude 7 comments on Sodom and Gomorrah, and other cities around them, as "having given themselves over to sexual immorality and having gone after strange flesh", clearly supporting the interpretation of God's judgment upon homosexuality.

---

[261] D. S. Bailey, (Homosexuality and the Western Christian Tradition), pages 3-5

Homosexuality is strongly condemned in the Mosaic Law. Leviticus 18:22 states, "You shall not lie with a male as with a woman; it is an abomination." Leviticus 20:13 says, "If a man lies with a male as with a woman, both of them have committed an abomination; they shall be put to death, their blood is upon them." The Hebrew word 'abomination' (toebah), used five times in Leviticus 18, is a term of strong disapproval, meaning literally something detestable and hated by God.[262]

Judges 19:16-21 has a similar story to that of Sodom and Gomorrah. A Levite is traveling with his concubine and is shown hospitality by an older man in Gibeah, located in the tribe of Benjamin. Some wicked men of the town of Gibeah came requesting sexual relationships with this Levite man. The concubine woman is given to the men and they abuse and rape her throughout the night, leading to her death.

We find New Testament references to homosexuality in three places: Romans 1:26, 27; 1 Corinthians 6:9-11; and, 1 Timothy 1:10.

Romans 1:26-27 specifically speaks of the subject of homosexuality. We must not lose sight of the context of these verses. When you read the whole passage of Scripture from Romans 1:18 to Romans 2:1, you find an extensive list of sins that brings all mankind under the righteous judgment of God. The apostle Paul speaks of man being totally inexcusable because of the fact that God has revealed himself sufficiently in His creation to make every man knowledgeable of God's existence and of God's power. The apostle Paul clearly teaches that the wrath of God is poured out upon all

---

[262] Gordon J. , Wenham, (The Book of Leviticus, Eerdman's Publishing, Grand Rapids, Michigan, 1979), page 259

mankind because they have "repressed the truth in unrighteousness" (verse 18), and "they did not glorify him as God, nor were thankful, but became futile in their thoughts, and their foolish hearts were darkened" (verse 21).

The apostle Paul, therefore, cannot be labeled a homophobe because he is speaking out against all wickedness and unrighteousness of mankind. We may label Paul a 'sinophobe', for he is speaking out against all sins and all unrighteousness. Because God is holy, He labels all that is contrary to His holy nature, sinful and wicked, deserving of both physical and spiritual death. Because every human being is born with a sinful nature, he inevitably sins against God. He cannot escape the fact that he also chooses to sin. The apostle states that men do not like to "retain God in their knowledge." Therefore, God gives them over "to a debased mind, to do those things which are not fitting; being filled with all unrighteousness, sexual immorality, wickedness, covetousness, maliciousness; full of envy, murder, strife, deceit, evil mindedness; they are whisperers, backbiters, haters of God, violent, proud, boasters, inventors of evil things, disobedient to parents, undiscerning, untrustworthy, unloving, unforgiving, unmerciful". (Romans 1:28-31).

When we come to the text of Romans 1:26-27, and when we approach it honestly, it very clearly teaches that homosexuality is regarded as sin by God. In fact, Paul the apostle, inspired by the Holy Spirit, labels it "vile passions" (NKJV) or "shameful lusts" (NIV). John Jefferson Davis comments on the meaning of these words in the original Greek language.

In verse 26, Paul uses the words 'pathe atimias', "shameful lusts," literally, "passions of dishonor." The term 'pathos' means "passion" or "passionate desire," the ungoverned aspect of evil desire. The word 'atimia' denotes "dishonor" or "disgrace."

In verse 27, he used the word 'exekauthesan', the aorist passive of 'ekkaio' "to set on fire"; Here, "to be consumed or to be inflamed." (It) means "shameless," "disgraceful"; "obscenity." Paul's moral judgment on such practices is clear.

It will not do to suggest that the apostle was condemning only "irresponsible" or "promiscuous" homosexual acts. Given the context in the passage, it is quite evident that homosexuality per se is contrary to the will of God."[263]

Paul also teaches us that homosexuality is against the nature of God's creation of male and female.

For this reason God gave them up to vile passions. For even their women exchanged the natural use for what is against nature. Likewise also the man, leaving the natural use of the woman, burned in their lust for one another, men with men committing what is shameful, and receiving in themselves the penalty of their error which was due.[264]

The 1 Corinthians 6:9-11 passage brings both judgment and hope to all sinners, including homosexual sinners and adulterous sinners. The gospel makes it very clear that no human being has any hope of forgiveness and eternal life without repenting and trusting in Jesus Christ as Savior and

---

[263] John Jefferson Davis, IBID, page 119
[264] Romans 1:26-27

Lord. It is only through His payment of our sin debt through His atoning death on the cross that we have any hope of escaping God's judgment and His wrath.

> Do you not know that the unrighteous will not inherit the kingdom of God? Do not be deceived. Neither fornicators, nor idolaters, nor adulterers, nor homosexuals, nor sodomites, nor thieves, nor covetous, nor drunkards, nor revilers, nor extortioners will inherit the kingdom of God. And such were some of you. But you were washed, but you were sanctified, but you were justified in the name of the Lord Jesus and by the Spirit of our God.[265]

Among the believers in the Corinthian church, there were those who, in their past, had been practicing homosexuality, and there were those who, in their past, had been committing other sexual sins. Paul clearly teaches that their lives had been transformed when they had come to Jesus Christ in repentance and faith. The secular society claims that homosexuality is simply another lifestyle and is inherited at birth. Therefore, they claim that it is impossible for a homosexual to change. This is refuted by the apostle Paul in this passage of Scripture. It is clear from Scripture that any sin is by our human choice. It is not a sufficient excuse before God, to claim "I couldn't help it. That's the way I am."

We make wrong sinful choices because we have a sinful nature. Jesus explains that it is because of our sinful hearts that we choose to sin. As Jesus was responding to the scribes and Pharisees, as they

---

[265] 1 Corinthians 6:9-11

complained about the disciples eating with unwashed hands, he said, "Not what goes into the mouth defiles a man; but what comes out of the mouth, this defiles a man." Jesus further explains to His disciples what he meant by this teaching. He said,

> Do you not yet understand that whatever enters the mouth goes into the stomach and is eliminated? But those things which proceed out of the mouth come from the heart, and they defile a man. For out of the heart proceed evil thoughts, murders, adulteries, fornications, thefts, false witness, blasphemies. These are the things which defile a man, but to eat with unwashed hands does not defile a man.[266]

Immorality includes much more than sexual sin. It includes any violation of God's moral code. However, the apostle Paul, commanded the Corinthian church to "Flee sexual immorality." He then clearly tells the Corinthian Christians that sexual immorality of any kind is in a special class of its own. "Every sin that a man does is outside the body, but he who commits sexual immorality sins against his own body."[267] The apostle Paul writes to the church at Thessalonica about the sanctified and pure sexual relationship between a husband and his wife.

> For this is the will of God, your sanctification: that you should abstain from sexual immorality; that each of you should know how to possess his own vessel in sanctification and honor, not in passion of lust, like the Gentiles who do not know God;

---

[266] Matthew 15:11, 17-20
[267] 1 Corinthians 6:18

that no one should take advantage of and defraud his brother in this matter, because the Lord is the avenger of all such, as we also forewarned you and testified. For God did not call us to uncleanness, but in holiness.[268]

It is sad to see many in our present day, who claim to be evangelical Christians, have changed their mind to endorse homosexual marriage. If you are one who has made that change, will you seek to honestly answer these penetrating questions?

How would you honestly use Scripture to make a biblical case for sexual activity between two persons of the same sex? How can you honestly use Scripture to show that this is a blessing to be celebrated rather than sinful behavior to be avoided? As you consider the historic position of the church and the almost universal disapproval of same-sex sexual activity, do you think you understand the teachings of the Bible more accurately than Augustine, Aquinas, Calvin, and Luther? When you stand before Christ Jesus on the judgment day, will you be ashamed that you rejected God's word in favor of the approval of the culture of this sinful world? Are you fearful of the reaction you will receive if you take your stand for truth?

How Should We Respond to Our Homosexual Neighbors?

The militant homosexual advocates will spin the truth of God's word in an effort to justify their sinful behavior. Dr. Joseph M. Stowell writes about 'Jesus in the spin zone . . .'

---

[268] 1 Thessalonians 4:3-7

To hear Rosie O'Donnell talk you'd hardly believe that Jesus is on the 'outs' in America. In fact, we hear His name spoken of frequently in admiring and embracing ways. It seems as though everyone wants Jesus in their parade. From gay activists to abortionists to religious leaders to politicians, making Jesus fit their agendas and flying His flag provides a guise of propriety and credibility.

Rosie recently outed herself as an avowed lesbian. Her first major crusade was to promote the adoption of children by gay parents. One testy news anchor talked her into one of the few interviews she granted after coming out of the closet. During the interview, she talked about the deep agony of her growing up years. She spoke of her new life as a liberating and satisfying replacement for the abuse of her past. I watched with great interest in utter amazement as the conversation continued.

The skilled, and obviously religiously savvy host, referring to the now-retracted statements from some religious leaders that 9/11 was partially caused by gays in America, asked Miss O'Donnell if she felt threatened by that sort of rhetoric. Her response was shocking. Basically, she said no, since she more than anyone understood the teachings of Jesus - namely love, kindness, compassion and understanding. When the intrigued interviewer pressed O'Donnell on whether she risked ultimate judgment from God because of her lifestyle, she calmly replied, "No." Her reason? After all, she had endured in her life, she felt convinced Jesus would smile on the fact that she could love at all.

As I sat silent, I thought to myself, "Jesus was being spun big time." He is either the Righteous One who will judge everyone, according to their works, or He is Rosie's Jesus who tolerantly and lovingly embraces her life choices regardless.[269]

The militant homosexual, who is fighting for the legitimacy and approval of his chosen lifestyle, will no doubt resist the Bible's message. However, the average homosexual neighbor is not on that cultural warpath. Therefore, do not bring up their chosen lifestyle as a topic of your conversation. However, if your homosexual neighbor brings up the topic and wants to know what your opinion is, you must share the truth with them. Make sure they understand that it is not your own opinion that matters. It is God's revealed word in the Bible that is important. The Bible tells us not only that homosexuality is a sin, but that all sexual behavior outside of the marriage of a man and a woman is sin.

Respond to them as you would respond to all neighbors. Love them and seek to show the love of Christ to them. Don't judge them simply on the basis of their homosexual behavior. Remember that "God did not send his Son into the world to condemn the world, but that the world through Him might be saved."[270] Don't be surprised or shocked when sinners act like sinners. When lost people act like lost people, we should not be alarmed. They are not our enemies, but they are souls for whom Jesus Christ died and rose again. So make sure that you respond to them with grace and truth, seeking to

---

[269] Joseph M. Stowell, The Trouble with Jesus (Moody publishers, Chicago, Illinois, 2003), pages 77-79
[270] John 3:17

meet their needs in the name of Jesus Christ, your Savior and Lord.

Seek opportunities to share the gospel message with them, just as you would with any other neighbor. Identify yourself with them, as sinners in the sight of God. All of us have sinned and come short of the glory of God. God sent His Son, Jesus Christ, to die on the cross for all of us sinners. He suffered and died, enduring hell itself for us, our rightful punishment, so that we may be forgiven and receive eternal life as a free gift. God expects all of us to repent from our sin, to turn to Jesus Christ, allowing Him to come into our lives and change us from the inside out. He loves us just the way we are, but He loves us too much to leave us that way.

Be sure to let them know that God does not ask us to change ourselves before we come to Him for His salvation. If we repent and come just as we are, sinners deserving of His punishment, He will grant His free gift of eternal life. He will make us new creatures with new hearts. He will put His Holy Spirit within us, and grant us His power to live in a way that pleases Him.

The Question of Abortion

On July 15, 2015, reports came through a video done undercover, that Planned Parenthood is harvesting organs from aborted babies and selling them to medical companies for research purposes. On the video, Dr. Deborah Nucatola, Senior Director of Medical Services for Planned Parenthood Federation of America, is shown casually discussing the grizzly procedure of removing seventeen week and older fetuses from the mother's body. As she casually eats her lunch and sips on her wine, she describes the procedure as they crush the head of the baby, then carefully manipulate their forceps on the thorax in order not to damage the baby's organs. Dr. Nucatola stated that her organization typically charges thirty to one hundred dollars 'per specimen' for fetal tissue it obtains by means of abortion. Many organizations, including government agencies, are promising an investigation. It is inconceivable that our federal government continues to fund this organization with millions of our tax dollars.

Subsequent videos continue to show doctors, working for Planned Parenthood, negotiating prices for baby parts obtained from abortions. Babies are being killed by the thousands in this United States of America. How ironic that we callously take the lives of babies and sell their organs, supposedly to save the lives of others, by enabling research with the parts of these murdered babies. How uncivilized and barbaric have we become as a nation!

Roe versus Wade, in 1973, officially approved the killing of babies under the guise of a woman's right to choose. The Supreme Court once again deconstructed the Constitution to rule that a woman has a right to control her own body. Those who justify abortion refuse to call the baby a live human being. They refer to the baby as the product of conception – POC - or the fetus. Since 1973, it is estimated that at least 63 million babies have been killed by legalized abortions. Pro-abortion advocates still refer to abortions as part of 'women's health care'.

Since 1973, scientific knowledge about the development of the baby during pregnancy has expanded by leaps and bounds. Ultrasounds and sonograms have given us the ability to track the development of the baby in the mother's womb.

The DNA, the informational map for each human being, is totally present at conception. Only those who blind themselves to the evidence will continue to say that this is not a live human baby.

The Mayo Clinic traces the development of the baby on their website. The following is just a small part of their presentation.[271]

> Weeks 1 and 2: Getting ready: It might seem strange, but you're not actually pregnant the first week or two of the time allotted to your pregnancy. Yes, you read that correctly!
>
> Conception typically occurs about two weeks after your last period begins. To calculate your due date, your health care provider will count ahead 40 weeks from the start of your last period. This means your period is counted as part of your pregnancy - even though you weren't pregnant at the time.
>
> Week 6: The neural tube closes: Growth is rapid this week. Just four weeks after conception, the neural tube along your baby's back is closing and your baby's heart is pumping blood.
>
> Basic facial features will begin to appear, including passageways that will make up the inner ears and arches that will contribute to the jaw. Your baby's body begins to take on a C-shaped curvature. Small buds will soon become arms and legs.

Pro-abortion advocates say that they defend the right of a woman to choose what she does with her

---

271   http://www.mayoclinic.org/healthy-lifestyle/pregnancy-week-by-week/in-depth/prenatal-care/art-20045302

body. A woman has a right and responsibility to control her body (as does a man have the right and responsibility to control his body) before conception, not afterwards. Once she becomes pregnant, her choice has been made. She then becomes accountable to society, and primarily to God, for the life that now exists within her body. America has become numb and calloused toward the value of human life. Our churches and our pastors need to stand up to this tragedy, this Holocaust going on in our nation.

The language of Scripture is not the language of modern science. It was not that God knew nothing about embryos, sperm and egg, zygotes or DNA; after all, He created us. But such language, if revealed to the Psalmist by the Holy Spirit, would have been irrelevant to the people of his day.

Listen to the Scriptures of the Old Testament as they describe the formation of a human baby. Psalms 139:13-16 says,

> For You formed my inward parts; You covered me in my mother's womb. I will praise You, for I am fearfully and wonderfully made; marvelous are Your works, and that my soul knows very well. My frame was not hidden from You, when I was made in secret, and skillfully wrought in the lowest parts of the earth. Your eyes saw my substance, being yet unformed. And in Your book they all were written, the days fashioned for me, when as yet there were none of them.

In Job 10:8-12, the suffering saint, Job, talks of God's wondrous work in creating him. Here God is pictured as the Master Craftsman molding a new human being in the womb.

Your hands have made me, and fashioned me, an intricate unity. Yet You would destroy me. Remember, I pray, that You have made me like clay. And will You turn me into dust again? Did You not pour me out like milk, and curdle me like cheese, clothe me with skin and flesh, and knit me together with bones and sinews? You have granted me life and favor, and your care has preserved my spirit.

The key issue in this whole debate is 'when does life begin?' Justice Blackmun's statement in the Roe Verses Wade decision causes one to question how such a learned man could think so illogically. He said, "We need not to resolve the question as to when life begins." C. Everett Koop, former United States Surgeon General, said: "When Mr. Blackmun said that the Court was not in a position to speculate on when life begins, he did us a great disservice. The Court really did decide when life begins in that it decided that life does not begin before live birth."[272]

Justice Blackmun wanted the issue to be a woman's right to control her body. If it is true that life begins at conception, then the woman does not have the right to abort the life of another human being who is presently dwelling in her womb.

The Scriptures teach that life begins at conception. The Scriptures teach that Adam and Eve were created as adult humans who were given the power and responsibility to reproduce. At Athens, Paul

---

[272] I gathered this quote from C Everett Koop from a newspaper article. I am not certain which newspaper carried the article, however, it probably was the St. Paul Pioneer Press, or the Minneapolis Tribune.

taught that all human beings come from one human father. Acts 17:26-28 says,

> And He has made from one blood every nation of men to dwell on all the face of the earth, and has determined their pre-appointed times, and the boundaries of their dwellings, so that they should seek the Lord, in the hope that they might grope for Him and find Him, though He is not far from each one of us; for in Him we live and move and have our being, as also some of your own poets have said, 'for we are also His offspring.'

The apostle Paul, in Romans 5:12-21, argues the point that each of us has inherited our sinful nature from Adam. The psalmist, David, speaks of this in Psalms 51:5. "Behold, I was brought forth in iniquity, and in sin my mother conceived me." If life does not begin until after live birth, how could the biblical writers state that our sinful nature is there from the time of conception?

The Holy Spirit was the agent by whom the Lord Jesus was conceived in Mary. Was He not a human baby until He was born alive? The baby, John, the Baptist, leaped for joy in his mother's womb, when Elizabeth heard the news from Mary of the coming Messiah. Surely this one who rejoiced so much over the news of the Messiah was not merely a fetus or product of conception, but a real living baby!

The word "brephos" is used in I Peter 2:2 to refer to a new born child. Dr. Luke uses the same word in Luke 18:15 (babies who were brought to Jesus) and exactly the same word in Luke 1:41, 44 to refer to John, the Baptist, still in Elizabeth's womb. Scientifically and medically, we know that when the sperm fertilizes the egg, twenty three sets of chromosomes unitedly contain every bit of that new human being. All that is 'you' was present at the moment of conception, undeveloped to be sure, but all contained in the intricate maps of the chromosomes and the DNA. Your physical features, your personality, your mind, your eternal soul, possessing an inherited sinful nature, were all there. How can we reach any conclusion from Scripture and science, other than that life begins at conception and therefore to abort a baby is to immorally murder another human being?

We as Bible believing Christians need to return to a solid commitment to God's moral standards when it comes to our sexuality and our sexual behavior. Abortion cannot be allowed to be a birth control method or a method of escaping the shame of lax moral standards. Nor can we cater to the selfish ambitions and whims of people who decide after pregnancy that the child will be a great inconvenience or hardship. We must continue to work for the reversal of the Roe verses Wade decision which is a horrible blight upon this nation. We must not grow weary of writing letters and protesting the shedding of innocent blood in our nation and in our world. We must call the United States of America to repent, and seek for the mercy and forgiveness of our God.

At the same time, we must offer forgiveness and the love of Christ to those who have had an abortion. It is a sin but it is not the unpardonable sin. Genuine repentance and faith in Jesus Christ and His blood shed on Calvary's cross brings forgiveness and freedom from all sin and guilt.

Standing For God and Truth

God's moral code involves much more than sexual morality. Christians are called to live pure and holy lives, to put off all the works of the flesh and the old nature. We are called to be salt and light in our world. We are to be a godly people who are living lives of integrity. We are to be honest, putting off greed and covetousness. We are to be compassionate and loving to all people, especially to the poor and needy, to orphans and widows.

Pastors must take up the challenge of the apostle Paul to Timothy: "Preach the word! Be ready in season and out of season. Convince, rebuke, exhort, with all long-suffering and teaching." [273]

Teach the people of God, those redeemed through the shed blood of the Savior and entrusted to you as your flock, to live the lifestyle of repentance. Teach them to stop loving the world and the things of the world. Teach them that repentance is a life to be lived, not simply a place to be visited occasionally.

Be faithful, stand up for God and his revealed word. Through the power and presence of the Holy Spirit in your life, lovingly preach the word of God. As the world's culture pressures you to conform to the world's system, be transformed by the power of the Spirit of God, renewing your mind and strengthening your spine. Paul tells us that we must be transformed in our lives and not let the world's system press us into its mold. [274]

As Paul challenged Timothy, "You, therefore, must endure hardship as a good soldier of Jesus Christ.

---

[273] 2 Timothy 4:2
[274] Romans 12:1-2

No one engaged in warfare entangles himself with the affairs of this life, that he may please him who enlisted him as a soldier."[275]

---

[275] 2 Timothy 2:3-4 and

Epilogue

Because you are reading this epilogue, I am almost certain that you have taken the time to read this book. I thank you for considering what I have felt led to write. I have prayed much as I have written. I have sought the Holy Spirit's leading in writing each chapter. I do not ask that you accept every idea that I've shared. I simply ask that the Holy Spirit will lead you to apply what is useful in bringing revival to you personally and to your church.

When Jesus was speaking some hard discipleship truths to the crowds who were following Him after they had been fed miraculously, many of His followers turned away and walked with Him no more. Jesus asked His twelve disciples, "Do you also want to go away?" Simon Peter answered Him, "Lord, to whom shall
we go? You have the words of eternal life. Also we have come to believe and know that You are the Christ, the Son of the living God."[276] A read through the Gospels makes it abundantly clear that Jesus was seeking genuinely obedient disciples, rather than the fickle crowds who were wanting His miracles to serve their selfish desires.

Pastor, don't be obsessed by the numbers game. Devote yourself to evangelism and lead your church to reach as many genuinely repentant sinners as possible. Disciple them to be devoted genuine followers of Jesus Christ who will stand when the fires of persecution descend upon us. Believe the word of God from cover to cover and do not compromise the truth of God's word. Preach the word of God in its entirety.

---

[276] John 6:66-69

As pastors of God's flock we must hold forth the truth of the word of God, preaching it with the authority that it possesses, because it is given by God Himself. Dr. Henry M. Morris III, says:

> Ezekiel faced a similar problem when God commissioned him to challenge the exiled Israelites to pay attention to the reason they were in exile and to God's promises of their future restoration. God warned Ezekiel that the message would be difficult to hear and even more challenging to embrace. In several places, God insisted that Ezekiel was to preach the message 'whether they hear or whether they refuse' (Ezekiel 2:5, 7; 3:11). Some were openly defiant, but more were generally accepting, encouraging others: "please come and hear what the word is that comes from the Lord." (Ezekiel 33:30). But they were merely listening to the pleasant 'sound' of godly words.

Morris, then quotes from Ezekiel 33:31-32:

> So they come to you as people do, they sit before you as My people, and they hear your words, but they do not do them; for with their mouth they show much love, but their hearts pursue their own gain. Indeed, you are to them as a very lovely song of one who has a pleasant voice and can play well on an instrument; for they hear your words, but they do not do them.

Morris continues:

> God's observation to Ezekiel is surely applicable today. Poll after poll has noted a slippage in the religious fervor in America.

241

Not only has the overall 'Christian' percentage slipped a few points, but more and more younger people are moving from identity with a recognized denomination (Baptist, Presbyterian, Catholic, etc.) to what has come to be called the 'nones' - those who refuse to be identified with any religious movement. Some might consider themselves 'Christian', and would not identify as Islamic or Hindu or another religion, but consider themselves to be 'spiritual.' One-fifth of the U. S. public - and a third of adults under 30 - are religiously unaffiliated today, the highest percentages ever in Pew Research Center polling.

It has been clear for some time, however, that the 'Christian' majority is Christian in name only. That is, they either have a family history of Christianity, or they themselves attend some church from time to time. Their religion is mostly an intellectual awareness, a superficial affirmation, or a pleasant assurance about their lifestyle or their life after death. They feel good if and when they think about Christianity, but most of their lives do not reflect any kind of commitment to following Christ or his commandments.[277]

This is the challenge to the 21st century evangelical church. As pastors, we must preach the word of God, anointed by the Holy Spirit. We must be living out genuine, biblical Christianity in our own lives. We must challenge professing Christians to become real disciples of Jesus Christ who display the walk in the Spirit daily. The apostle Paul, in Romans 8,

---

[277] Dr. Henry M. Morris III, Article: Sounds of Music, Words of Truth (Acts & Facts magazine, published by Institute for Creation Research, Dallas, Texas August 2015, pages 6-7

writes clearly, describing how the true believer walks in the Spirit of God.

> For the law of the Spirit of life in Christ Jesus has made me free from the law of sin and death. For what the law could not do in that it was weak through the flesh, God did by sending His own Son in the likeness of sinful flesh, on account of sin: He condemned sin in the flesh, that the righteous requirement of the law might be fulfilled in us who do not walk according to the flesh but according to the Spirit. For those who live according to the flesh set their minds on the things of the flesh, but those who live according to the Spirit, the things of the Spirit . . . For if you live according to the flesh, you will die; but if by the Spirit you put to death the deeds of the body, you will live. For as many as our led by the spirit of God, these are sons of God.[278]

We live in desperate times. The Western world church is in a rapid decline, while the church in much of the rest of the world is experiencing the fresh winds of the Holy Spirit. While there are a few exceptions, most of America's evangelical churches profess to be alive, but inwardly are very sick spiritually. We are relying on our own strength, rather than seeking the power of God to move in our midst. The churches are much like Ephraim, as described by the prophet Hosea.

> Ephraim has mixed himself among the peoples; Ephraim is a cake unturned. Aliens have devoured his strength, but he does not know it; yes, gray hairs are here and there on him, yet he does not know it. And the pride of

---

[278] Romans 8:2-5; 13-14

Israel testifies to his face, but they do not return to the Lord their God, nor seek him.[279]

Dr. Jim Denison shared the following evaluation of the state of the world-wide church.

More people are coming to Christ today than ever before in Christian history. According to David Barrett's World Christian Encyclopedia, more than 82,000 come to Christ every day. Other scholars put the number as more than a million a week.

South Korea is one-third to one-half born-again Christian. Yoido Full Gospel Church has nearly a million members. Hillsong worship is transforming Australia and worship around the world. Brazil will be one-half evangelical Christian by 2025. Ninety percent of the people in southern Nigeria were in church last Sunday. When I was in Beijing, I was told that 100,000 people come to Christ every day in the People's Republic of China. More Muslims have come to Christ in the last fifteen years than the previous fifteen centuries. I've met them in Bangladesh and Cairo and across the Middle East.

Now to the bad news: we are not seeing this awakening in the West. In fact, the opposite is happening. Most of us remember when the church was central to our culture. Stores were closed on Sundays. Billy Graham was always named to the "most admired" list. However, in recent decades, we have moved from

---

[279] Hosea 7:8-10

central to marginal, from significant to irrelevant.

A recent Harris Poll conducted a large survey of religious beliefs in France, Germany, Great Britain, Italy, Spain, and the U.S. The results: only 62% in Italy; 48% in Spain; 41% in Germany; 35% in England; and 27% in France believe in any form of a supreme being.

In Great Britain today, there are four times as many Muslims attending mosque on Friday as Christians attending worship on Sunday. Twenty-five percent of Brussels is Muslim. Fifty-four million Muslims live in Europe; their numbers will continue to increase due to immigration and high birth rates. Of David Barrett's 82,000 conversions a day, only 6,000 are in Western Europe and North America, combined.[280]

We have beautiful, functional church buildings. We have the latest of technology at our fingertips. We've contrived countless new methods to seek to reach the unchurched. We have more mega-churches in America than ever in our history. With all of this affluence and methodology, the number of evangelicals in America is decreasing in number. The secularists and the atheists are an increasing percentage in America.

What is missing in our Western world churches? Why is it that we have so little power? Why is evangelism in our Western world and in Europe so

---

[280] Jim Denison, (Denison Forum on Truth and Culture, A Surprising Strategy for Reaching Our Culture! February 3 2015)

anemic when compared to the evangelical church in Asia, Africa, and many countries in South America?

Listen to the message to the church of the Laodiceans, the last of the seven churches of Revelation.

> And to the angel of the church of the Laodiceans, these things says the Amen, the Faithful and True Witness, the Beginning of the creation of God: 'I know your works, that you are neither cold nor hot. I could wish you were cold or hot. So then, because you are lukewarm, and neither cold nor hot, I will vomit you out of my mouth. Because you say, I am rich, have become wealthy, and have need of nothing - and do not know that you are wretched, miserable, poor, blind, and naked - I counsel you to buy from me gold refined in the fire, that you may be rich; and white garments, that you may be clothed, that the shame of your nakedness may not be revealed; and anoint your eyes with eye salve, that you may see. As many as I love, I rebuke and chasten. Therefore be zealous and repent. Behold, I stand at the door and knock. If anyone hears my voice and opens the door, I will come into him and dine with him, and he with Me. To him who overcomes I will grant to sit with Me on My throne, as I also overcame and sat down with My Father on His throne. He who has an ear, let him hear what the Spirit says to the churches.'[281]

Our God has become small in our spiritual eyes. The psalmist David, observing the stars, the sun and the moon, simply with his naked eyes was

---

[281] Revelation 3:14-22

overwhelmed at the immensity and the greatness of Almighty God who had created it all. In our 21st century world, with all the accomplishments of science, we are able to see into the far-off distances of creation. With microscopes, we are able to explore the intricate complex world of the cell. Our minds are blown away by what we have discovered. The intricacies of the human body demonstrate to us the greatness of our Almighty Creator God. Such knowledge, while still very limited in its scope, ought to cause us to fall on our knees and recognize our insignificance in a much greater way than King David ever could. "What is man that you are mindful of him, and the Son of Man, that you visit him?"[282]

Jesus Christ said to Peter, in Matthew 16:18, "I will build my church, and the gates of Hades shall not prevail against it." He has chosen to work through believers - common, ordinary people. However, He will only show His power through believers who walk humbly and depend totally upon Him. He honors those who really believe His words, ". . . without Me, you can do nothing!"[283] The work of building His church is supernatural work and is only accomplished through the supernatural power of His Holy Spirit through clean, humble, yielded, anointed servants. This is why the apostle Paul could so boldly say, "I can do all things through Christ who strengthens me."[284]

It is time for the churches to heed the voice of the psalmist in Psalm 46:10 when he wrote, "Be still, and know that I am God; I will be exalted among the nations, I will be exalted in the earth." The words, 'be still' are from the Hebrew word 'raphah'

---

282 Psalm 8:4
283 John 15:5
284 Philippians 4:13

which is often translated 'cease'. Strong's concordance gives other meanings, such as 'to abate, be faint, be feeble, be weak'.[285] It is time for us to cease depending upon our own efforts and our own programs to build the church of Jesus Christ. It is time for us as believers, and church leaders, to get a new understanding of Almighty God. It is time for us to cease all of our frantic efforts to bring about the kingdom of God on earth. It is time to seek His face and His favor. When we are willing to humbly acknowledge that we need the supernatural working of Almighty God in our midst, then we will see the powerful working of our God in building His church. The most urgent need of the church and her leaders today is to get desperate in seeking and experiencing the power of God once again.

Oh Lord, send a great revival to us in America! Be merciful toward us who call ourselves by Your Name, Lord Jesus Christ! Forgive us for our forms of religion that are without Your power and Your blessing. Cleanup our lives. Restore our heart's devotion. Wean us from our worldly materialistic entanglements. Cure us from our luke-warmness and our mediocrity. Give us a renewed passion for your holiness and the glory of Your Name. Restore our faith and our commitment to You, our Almighty God, and to Your kingdom's cause.

Ephesians 3:20-21: "Now to Him who is able to do exceedingly abundantly above all that we ask or think, according to the power that works in us, to Him be glory in the church by Christ Jesus to all generations, forever and ever. Amen."

---

[285] Strong's Concordance, Hebrew and Chaldee Dictionary, page 110, number 7503.

Made in the USA
Charleston, SC
21 February 2016